POWER
to COACH

Hardcover ISBN: 978-1-955342-73-5.
Paperback ISBN: 978-1-955342-74-2.

Published by Holon Publishing. Printed by Ingram Lightning Source.

www.holon.co

HOLON
PUBLISHING

Testimonials

"Simply put, Dan is a superstar. He is an exceptional leader, coach and supporter of every member of our Vistage group. After every meeting with him, I return to my desk enriched, with a better perspective and with more confidence in my decisions and direction. He is a valuable source and helps me exchange ideas that move me closer to achieving my goals. I am lucky to be in his circle and value my time with him immensely."

—*Jacqui Lewis, former President, Serial Entrepreneur, Audley Travel US, Inc.*

"June has this uncanny ability to switch from a conersation that touches the depths of your human spirit in one moment to holding a room-full of C-suite leaders to task in this next moment in a way that simultaneously clarifies your own place in humanity and the next immediate steps to drive organizational change. The ease with which she wields her warm and connecting present is impressive in almost any situation and across very diverse audiences. Grounded in her own commitment to excavating the best in other people, watching her navigate group dynamics is akin to watching a master craftsman weave an ornate tapestry."

—*Barton Cutter, Principal, Cutter's Edge Consulting*

"I took the Power to Coach program, and it was immensely powerful to me. So why, why would I take a coaching class when I coach over 40 CEO's a month? It was pretty simple to me. I want to be better. I want to learn as much as I can about helping great leaders become great coaches within their organizations. The program allowed me the space to stop being the coach, and be the student again, to absorb great content presented in the right context. It was fun, informative, hard, and insightful. I use much of my learning every day now. I highly recommend you give this a try."

—Nancy Babine Kucinski, Former CEO, Executive Coach, Vistage.

"June is an incredibly talented executive coach. She brings her talent and experience to every interaction, and helps her clients identify their strengths and key areas to focus on to keep improving. I worked with June for several quarters, and she helped me navigate and overcome key challenges, while always helping to shine the light on my strengths and successes.

I would highly recommend June for any team. She is an extraordinary leader, great listener, and always humble about the contributions she makes. She truly impacted my life and career path, and I will be forever grateful for her kindness and tough love."

—Cecilia Hoyt, Risk Management Executive

"I have pursued self-mastery for a long time, and I have had an executive coach for about 6 years. I am a big fan of coaching and jumped at the opportunity to learn the skill. It made intuitive sense to me that it could be a huge

tool for a business leader. However, in the program, I discovered that old habits die hard. I was far more comfortable in the director/supervisor role - teaching and telling others what to do. Learning to spot coaching opportunities and how to shift into the coaching posture has expanded my range as a leader, and I am loving it. Empowering others is a hoot!"

—*Charlie Saponaro, CEO, MRA.*

"I have had the great pleasure to work with June as I transitioned into two different senior leadership roles. Her guidance, insight and knowledge helped me focus on and execute a challenging leadership role during a period of tremendous professional and corporate change. Importantly, she helped me utilize my strengths, and compensate for my weaknesses, while always maintaining compassion and professionalism. Her calm demeanor, sharp analysis and deep understanding of corporate organization, plus tremendous insight to human behavior, allowed me to devise a leadership plan, implement the plan and remain sane during the process! June was invaluable to me over the past 12 months, and will help me and my career for the rest of my life."

—*George B., Investment Strategist*

TABLE OF CONTENTS

Introduction: How Leaders Who Coach are at the Future of Business

"The things we fear most in organizations—fluctuations, disturbances, imbalances—are the primary sources of creativity."

Margaret Wheately

In the corporate world, "more" is a word freighted with an awesome amount of expectation and responsibility.

What is a CEO traditionally tasked to do?

Find more clients or customers.

Get more out of the team.

Generate more revenue.

"More" has been grafted into the DNA of American business. In hiring. In promoting. In firing. In how organizations are evaluated for investment or for sale. If you're an up-and-coming star in your industry, you've traditionally evaluated opportunities based on "more."

More responsibility?

More opportunity?

More compensation?

All of this would have looked like Nirvana to Frederick Winslow Taylor, the genius mechanical engineer who came up with the concept of "scientific management" at the beginning of the 20th century. Taylor had invented a system for processing metal at much higher rates that made him a fortune, and he applied that same developmental mind to everything from the sports he played to the way he managed the employees at his firm. He noticed that the racquets he used to play tennis were wildly inconsistent. He invented his own, and won the first national doubles championship. He did the same thing with this golf equipment, and invented clubs that were so superior that the game's governing body ruled that using them was like cheating and banned them.

In managing employees, he determined that a worker—to be at his highest and best use—must be at one with his (and it was almost always a "his") machine—with no wasted time or less than full-out effort. His revolutionary efficiency testing boiled corporate performance down to cold, hard numbers—and literally gave birth to management training as a field of study. Harvard's business school opened in 1908, with "Taylorism" at its core.

There's no arguing with the numbers.

The United States became the towering financial capital of the world by the second decade of the 20th century. During World War II, we were the Arsenal of Democracy, marshaling enormous natural and organizational resources to build millions of guns, tanks, and planes. Through the 1950s and 1960s, American companies created the vast economic, industrial, and intellectual infrastructure that made us the richest, most influential country on the planet.

In fact, the average person reading this book right now has more earning potential, more access to food, more leisure time, and more ability to communicate with friends and colleagues than any person in the history of the planet—not to mention more computing superpower in the form of a smartphone than was available to send the first men to the moon.

More, indeed.

But, just like Frederick Taylor was responding to the tenor of his times in the 1890s, so are we. When Taylor worked for Bethlehem Steel, three percent of people ages 18-21 attended college. More than ten percent of the adult population was illiterate, and many who were literate were recent immigrants from central and Southern Europe who were literate in a different language. At the time, with the arrival of the industrial revolution, a reductive approach to managing the workforce was an adequate solution—but not necessarily a humane approach.

Today, we're experiencing social, financial, and cultural forces unlike any we've ever seen. Not only is the world intimately connected in a new way through digital communication and social media, but we're also experiencing a fundamental change in the relationship between employer and employee. For us to thrive, we need to understand and embrace a new approach.

For decades, leaders learned from experience and from business school the command and control tactics that treated employees as numbers in a ledger or on a spreadsheet. In other words, people were seen simply as units of production—assets to be deployed and used until they needed to be replaced, just like a piece of machinery.

It's no wonder, then, that employees began operating like mercenaries, putting their own needs before those of the company—even if that was at odds with their employers.

The paradigm is shifting. The organizations that will thrive will be ones who recognize the difference between managing—something done with assets and processes—and coaching people and teams. Leaders who can see this shift and embrace it—and coach others through it—are leading a business revolution unlike any other, because it is forcing a new truce between employee and employer.

To surf the wave of complexity and chaos we are experiencing, we need to not just be a team of agile, adaptable, and distributed contributors. We need those specific traits and skills to be foundational and instinctive in the culture—traits and skills that are highly relational and synergistic. This leads to a work culture that is continually self-organizing—the hallmark of the new and more sustainable business model. Organizations are spending millions of dollars to develop what they believe are agile leaders. To shift priority from processes and tools to individuals and relationships.

Coaching, as you will learn more about in this book, is a critical part of this evolution. It is one of many forms of leadership that helps others change and grow. It is broadly applicable, and is as relevant to a parent, friend, or colleague as it is to a CEO. It is also a tool of both power and nuance—a palette of colors in the hands of a master—for those who decide to use the tool and hone the skill. This is why we have written this book.

The tools you'll acquire in Power to Coach are the ones that are already becoming the standard for high-achieving leaders and organizations. Instead of using brute force and command and control, leaders who coach are catching the wave and discovering that empowering teams to self-organize and grow is a true lever—a force multiplier. We are working with the power of the collective changes that are always transforming the world, rather than wasting energy resisting that inevitable evolution.

In the hands of a senior leader—one who sees potential in others and the power of healthy relationships for all stakeholders in an organization—coaching can be a long lever that creates a sustainable culture where people love their work.

By learning how to coach your leaders, you are not only modeling life-long learning and personal growth, you are also learning how to intentionally help your leaders to step into their potential. Few things in life generate more joy—for both coach and coachee. As you can imagine, this dance creates work that people love and organizations where people thrive.

The time is now, and this book is the tool you need.

Why?

The truth is that there's so much information and stimulus out there that it's impossible for us to sort it out in the way somebody could conceivably have done so even 20 years ago. Recall of data isn't a separator. Sensing what is emerging and committing to an action before we know exactly what needs to happen *is*. Coaching is about helping others remain in the flow as they continue to learn and adapt on the fly—which is the reality of our reality, so to speak!

Brain scientists, sociologists, futurists, and other experts in human development are plotting the story of the "whole human"—the energy multiplier that comes when we embrace the wonderfully diverse skill set each contains and create environments that help people grow and transform—emerging into their full potential. When this happens, our work becomes more than "work." It becomes a source of meaning and belonging.

What is belonging? Belonging is about the fit between oneself and a setting. When you belong, you feel emotionally connected, welcomed, included, and satisfied in your relationships. Belonging means you're with a group that accepts you for who you are—because of who you are. You're with others to whom you have a deep connection. You have a mutual trust, and you're comfortable expressing your thoughts and opinions. You understand how things work within a given setting, feel treated equally, and perceive you can influence decisions. When people find belonging, they feel safe, seen, and useful.

Belonging is vital for society, and unlocks the door that reveals a rich, sustainable, high-performing culture.

At the core? More.

We know that as humans, the "more" we want goes beyond financial rewards and titles. It's about finding what moves you and drives you, and attaching yourself to a role and a team that activates those movers and drivers. The new "more" can be stimulated and shaped by coaching—which, in its simplest form, is a strikingly effective and engaging way to help others change, grow, and find their sense of belonging.

The new-generation CEO/leader is one that will recognize those factors on his or her own path. After all, you have most likely personally experienced coaching in the form of mentorship from colleagues who have helped accelerate your trajectory. So, you also understand the value that comes from coaching others within the organization into their own emergence. You see one important, fundamental truth: Great leaders grow more great leaders.

By emergence, we are simultaneously referring to potential and sets of behaviors in a complex, adaptive system such as a team or organization that isn't present as an individual working alone. We will unpack the concept of emergence more thoroughly in Chapter 3.

This book is designed to help those on this journey—either as a prospective coach or one who is looking to get more from coaching.

To be clear, this book is designed for those who:

- Lead high-performing teams.
- Are accomplished (or have the ambition to be) at far more than making a profit.
- Carry a broad set of values that extend well beyond the walls of the organization to the community and the world.
- Have an ample dose of desire and passion for more, including learning how to lead to their full potential.
- Are life-long learners.

Accordingly, the **purpose** of this book is to begin to teach you how to coach, and help the people you lead to continually blossom.

Emergence and self-organizing principles, as you may have already noticed, are the concepts at the heart of the Power to Coach.

Emergence is inseparable from the concept of synergy–when the whole is greater than the sum of the parts. The "greater than" is the emergence. It is the magic in the formula–the rabbit pulled from the magician's hat. It is that seemingly intangible thing that the underdog team possesses when it pulls off the "impossible" victory over a "better" team. To be more precise, the emergent quality of a team is less about the particles (players) and the whole (the team) than it is about the larger *system* of team *AND* players. It's the magic that happens when well-constructed teams build the trust and safe space that lets players cohere into an indivisible unit. The emergence is a new quality that only exists when parts cohere, or come together. Without teams, there is no game. There is no business!

As you will read later, self-organization describes the behavior of systems thrown into change and finding solutions to evolve. Emergence and self-organization are abundant, fundamental processes in nature, and should be in your business as well.

Are you ready to learn how to do that?

Chapter 1: Coaching Emergent Leadership—A Framework

"When a system is far from equilibrium, small islands of coherence in a sea of chaos have the capacity to lift the entire system to a higher order."

Chemist and Nobel Laureate, Illya Prigogine

There's a freedom and a joy to something when you refer to it as "natural." It's easy. It feels good.

Why is that?

It's because–instead of fighting against our basic wiring—we're using the entire suite of powerful, intellectual, emotional, and relational tools we have to *flow*.

Like all other complex and open systems in nature, we're pulsing through discernable stages—and we're sharing energy and information with other open systems that have the same basic features. We exist within a system of systems—which means we're all interconnected and working both independently <u>and</u> together in a continuous pattern. In fact, as humans, we're hard-wired for this connection and interconnection. It's a fundamental part of our evolution and survival.

Our introduction to this idea—and its implications in the worlds of coaching and leadership—came in the 1990s, when we first read two seismic books about systems thinking: Margaret J. Wheatley's "Leadership and the New Science: Learning About Organization from an Orderly Universe" and Peter Senge's "The 5th Discipline: The Art and Practice of Learning Organizations." Those texts resonated with our own felt experience with life, and sent us on a journey toward leadership and coaching that we'll describe in more detail below.

The "big bang" event for our work together came during the beginning stages of COVID in 2020. Like the rest of the world, we were worried about a lot of things— what would happen to the economy, how governments would respond to this threat, and what it meant for everyone from entrepreneurs trying to get started as the world turned upside down, to families with two working parents who now needed to figure out how to be schoolteachers for their young children.

In the search to find his bearings, Dan read far and wide, and I stumbled on a website that detailed how a particular agency was helping care for patients suffering from post-traumatic stress by applying many of the self-organizing principles you're going to be reading about on the next pages. I was transfixed, and I immediately grasped how this would impact our work—and my clients.

With the help of marketing professional Liz Taylor and Herculiz, her Austin-based firm, I built the diagram below, Phases of a Complex System, which became a document that many of my clients used to help their firms orient themselves within the new normal.

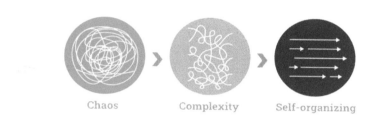

The first time we saw this completed diagram, we felt an ease that we hadn't experienced in a long time—since before the pandemic started. We could see where we were on the continuum, and we could also see where we were headed.

We would move from chaos to complexity, and eventually accelerate into self-organization on our path to emergence as we learn and adapt, becoming something new and different.

We weren't the only ones who responded to this frame. Our clients almost universally responded the same way. It gave them context—a sense that in the natural course of events, systems are always toggling into and out of equilibrium. Chaos and self-organization are inevitable parts of this cyclical and relentless journey in and out of equilibrium.

Why is this so important?

Because, whether we like it or not (or accept it or not!) we're all in this soup together.

Not only that, by definition, we're all interconnected—systems within systems. What we do impacts the rest of the "whole." Anything new we learn or experience changes the spin, so to speak.

Think about what might be the three most dominant "systems" in your own life: yourself, your family, and your work. What happens to you within one of those systems inevitably impacts the other systems. And, of course, you're not the only one changing and experiencing something new and different. Each other actor or system in the mix has its own constantly evolving and interdependent script.

Growth and change are constant—making it incumbent on us to develop an effective framework to deal with that reality. If we fail to conceive of a life that is in harmony and at peace with the flow of nature, life will always be overwhelming and frustrating. This applies to the business setting as well.

WHY SHOULD THIS MATTER TO YOU?

What becomes possible when you have a better, more satisfying way to navigate these realities - both in life and in business? What kind of leader will you be when you live and thrive in the moment, ready to adapt and ride more freely through the chaos and complexity of this ever-changing environment? How can coaching help you supercharge your organization and seed it with other leaders who coach?

We see you.

It's important to note that Power to Coach—and the kind of coaching we practice and teach—is not simply triage for executives who are struggling in their work or home lives. Coaching isn't counseling, and it's not remedial education. In fact, it's not mentorship or even consulting. An ideal coaching relationship in this world isn't a session where I (as the coach) listen to your issues and tell you what I would do if I were in your shoes—or evaluate your prospective solution and tell you if I think it'd work based on my own business experience.

Leadership coaching is partnership—a moderated discovery process that leads to insight, choice, and purposeful action. It is led by questions and thrives in the chaos and complexity that ultimately leads teams and individuals to self-organizing behaviors, relationships, skills, tools, and innovations. Effective leadership helps teams and individuals to differentiate and integrate their own experiences as they adapt and accelerate with the next new surprise.

This kind of coaching starts first with your relationship with yourself—which always translates into gaining more insight into your relationship with others. You become more effective at taking responsibility for creating your world, with your relationship to others firmly in mind, and the people around you will experience you differently.

Of course, coaching and being coached are different things, but the overwhelmingly positive feedback we had working with our most coachable clients was that they wanted to learn how to form a productive coaching relationship with somebody else on their team. They wanted to coach!

In other words, coaching your leaders is an integral part of the leadership calculus: Get coached, learn to coach, and then coach the leaders around you.

Because we were having this conversation so often, we decided to write this book as a guide for that experience. As we built out the outline, we field-tested all of the concepts in three cohorts of 30 CEO clients we brought together in a virtual learning environment. The feedback strongly suggests that the group learning format—and the content in this book—resonates.

Before we go further, it's worth a short detour to take a deeper dive into the concepts of leadership and coaching as we use them in this book.

LEADERSHIP

Leadership, as we use it, is simple to understand and therefore easily leveraged into your organization.

Leaders choose to take responsibility for creating their world, and anyone can choose to be a leader.

With this definition, two questions follow.

Who do I choose to be?

What is my Work?

Notice the potency of agency in the definition - *taking responsibility and creating my world!*

Consider this question: What in your life do you have the most control over? Note your answer before I give mine.

<u>Me! Myself!</u>

That's right, there is nothing over which I have as much direct control as myself. And the same goes for you. Because of this answer, it is our position that self-mastery is rule #1 in our leadership approach. This said, here is a big caveat which goes to one of the deeper mysteries of life. The separate self - the notion that I have complete and total autonomy - is an illusion, a dangerous one. The type of self-mastery to which we explicitly refer to is what could be called reciprocal self-mastery. As I master self, I learn to appreciate and honor myself for who I am and who I am becoming, which comes with a potent dose of grounding and awe. This simply means I am trusting myself to be genuine and authentic and building a sense of self-authority. All this leads to learning to connect more deeply with who I am and to be kind to myself. Harsh judgment of self diminishes the goodness that translates to others. Self-mastery is the best opportunity to study humanity directly. The better I understand myself, the better I can relate to others and contribute to others. And this is how it reciprocates. Any lessons that I learned about myself lead to increased empathy and compassion for others. Self-mastery, in other words, is also the first step in mastering how to connect, to creating a sense of belonging for self and for others, which clearly demonstrates the primacy of relationships in all that we do as both leader and coach.

On the next page is a dimensional diagram that helps to build the rich context of leadership and how coaching and leadership are related. You will see how and when coaching is leadership and leadership is coaching.

The heart of the context of leadership is leadership from <u>within</u>; as we've already discussed, this includes self-awareness, self-knowledge, self-authority, self-mastery, and self-compassion. Leadership emerges from within us—who we choose to be, and what we choose to do (our work).

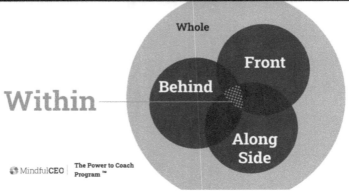

Adapted from the work of Henry and Karen Kimsey-House.

At the same time, we are a core element of the interconnected ecosystems of which humans are an integrated part. The diagram illustrates the ecosystems as a <u>whole</u>. We are in fact parts of multiple systems within systems. Think of being part of a leadership team, which is part of an organization, which is part of a community, which is part of a nation, which is part of humanity on Earth, which is part of all the natural systems on Earth and in the Universe. All of these are part of the Whole, and cannot be separated from the Whole. This is what we mean by *Leaders choose to take responsibility for creating their world*. Each action chosen is informed by the whole - the ecosystem(s) in which we are operating—and in turn influences the whole—creating the outcomes that we seek to create. There will be times, of course, when our impact does not match our intentions. When that happens, we must also take responsibility, then choose new actions to create more outcomes. We will explore this concept much more fully in the next chapter.

Leadership from the <u>front</u> is perhaps the form of leadership with which we are most familiar, and most often taught in business school. Leadership is commonly defined as the art of motivating a group of people to act toward achieving a common goal. Methods for leading from the front may include developing and communicating a strategy and obtaining and distributing the resources needed to accomplish a task. We see images of leaders at the front lines, leading their teams toward a vision the leader has created. This type of leadership is useful; however, it is often overused, and may be limited in vision based on the leader's individual experience, perspectives, and biases. When leaders see themselves as the director or solutions provider or point person, they are envisioning leadership from the front.

In our more global economy, leading <u>alongside</u> others in a truly collaborative way allows for new perspectives and vision. Leading alongside is the engine of co-creation. It is a force multiplier. As authors of this book we have chosen to lead alongside each other to bring the Power to Coach Program™ and this book to life, while also running our own independent businesses. By choosing to lead alongside, operate collaboratively, leverage each other's strengths, and compensate for our lesser strengths, we create stronger results and have a greater impact on the world. Our collaboration requires that we each hold both independent and shared visions, hold each other accountable to achieving those visions, push and pull each other to stay on course, and find that our ability to lead alongside each other is an exponential multiplier. Our relationship requires vulnerability, transparency, authenticity, and courage, which builds intimacy and trust. We must attend to our self-interests and shared interests, be reliable and accountable.

Leading from <u>behind</u> is perhaps one of the most misunderstood and underutilized forms of leadership, and we would argue is the leadership stance most called for in the world today. It is the leadership stance from which we grow other leaders—looking over their shoulders to see their vision of what they choose to create in the world, having their backs by helping them see what's ahead of them, anticipating and strategizing how to navigate potential obstacles on their own with our support and encouragement. Leaders who grow new leaders as a means of crafting their own succession understand what it means to lead from behind.

Coaching is woven throughout this understanding of dimensional leadership, and perhaps lives predominantly in the posture of leadership from behind.

COACHING

Coaching is a powerful form of leading from behind. Leaders who learn when and how to coach, lead from behind when applying coaching skills. Coaching is designed to help people uncover their internal motivation and inspiration to change, and to develop the skills and behaviors that improve confidence, competence, and ultimately performance. Great leaders grow more leaders. Coaching is one of the most dynamic modalities we know of to unlock potential in others.

There are qualities and traits – ways of 'being' an effective leader-coach – that combine with the 'doing' of coaching that create the desired outcomes. You will notice these ways of 'being' are all coming from the leader within, while the actions and skills of coaching are being applied from the posture of leading from behind.

- **Self-awareness** – the ability to acknowledge and monitor one's own personal biases, beliefs, attitudes, and reactions, and the potential impact of them on the conversation, on the coachee, and on the environment in which we are operating.
- **Presence** – the discipline of giving one's full, focused attention to the coachee and to

the moment; reducing or eliminating external distractions while paying attention to the overall flow of the conversation and noticing any energetic shifts within the conversation.

- **Integrity** – the ability to directly express, with respectful honesty, what is observed and/or sensed; the ability and willingness to openly admit when mistakes and/or errors in judgment or process has occurred, and then do what is needed to fix it.
- **Empathy** – the ability to understand and be with any underlying emotions present within the coachee, while simultaneously serving as objective witness to the coachee.
- **Intuition** – the ability to access your "gut reactions" or "instincts" to reveal what may be invisibly impacting a coachee and share them without attachment to being right.
- **Curiosity** – the ability to listen attentively to what is said and unsaid (not just in words but in silences, body language, and patterns over time), explore without making assumptions and ask questions from the real perspective of "not knowing".

The 'doing' of coaching is, in its most basic form, these four actions:

- Listening to understand.
- Asking questions powerfully and with authentic curiosity.
- Challenging and supporting.
- Establishing accountability.

This short list of core coaching skills belies how difficult they can be to use effectively. It is the empowered combination of doing and being that unlocks effective coaching.

Leadership is quite simply getting others to follow you and work toward achieving your vision. Great leaders choose to take responsibility for creating their world, finding their potential in the emerging future, and helping other leaders to do the same. Leadership starts from within and is always done in relationship to the whole – others, teams, organizations, industries, countries, cultures – the world.

Effective leadership truly needs to be multi-dimensional. From a place of self-knowing and expanded awareness of the whole in which we are operating, we may then choose to lead others from the front (ensuring we are attending to true followership in the process – a component all too often missed), lead alongside (in true partnership or collaboration with another, supporting a shared vision and each other) or lead from behind (as mentor, coach, or ally to other leaders who are leading from the front).

Our intention is to expand your capacity as a leader to hold self, others, and the context all at once, and to surf the emergent wave through chaos to complexity and ultimately to self-organization. Then, to learn and apply core coaching skills and ways of being to lead others to surf the emergent wave themselves, growing from the process.

Dan's life as a leader, father, husband, receiver of coaching, and coach is a story about the powerful connection between coaching and leadership to which you may identify.

Dan believes leaders are made. It is a skill—though it is more about who you are than what you do. Accordingly, it is an essential skill that you can hone and develop through your entire professional life.

He initially learned this the hard way. Dan was an athlete all his life—good enough to be the captain and leading performer for almost every team of which he was a member. When he was finally coached by someone who had more than rudimentary skills and charisma, he absolutely thrived. But those experiences were few and far between, and it took him until long into his professional career to receive truly elite coaching. The speed at which it helped him untangle what he thought were intractable problems blew his mind. Coaching became an accelerant for everything he was doing—both professionally and personally.

In the early 2000s, Dan shifted from tax law to private wealth planning, and in the midst of this transition he discovered a startling statistic. For most of his clients, upwards of 85 percent of their wealth was tied up in their business. Very few of them had any idea how to unlock that wealth, although they almost universally expected to have some kind of undetermined "wealth-creating" exit event in the future.

Dan began holding a series of round-table events with these clients to try to bring a sense of order and preparation for these exits, and those events eventually turned into a business. The Exit Planning Exchange (XPX) was created as a community of interdisciplinary advisors who help owners of privately-held businesses plan for succession and exit. The Exit Planning Exchange is an intentional collaboration of the interdisciplinary professions who come alongside business owners throughout the life cycle of a business from starting, to managing, to growing, to selling businesses and managing the emergent wealth upon a sale. The vision is to help business owners to optimize the journey. The organization is thriving to this day, with thousands of members and 20 chapters around the United States.

Dan's second-ever professional coach was a woman named Cindy Schumacher—who was a business coach focused on branding positioning and sales. She asked him a question that stopped him. He literally felt it in his gut.

"Dan, why don't you trust yourself to be yourself?" she asked him.

The question landed so hard, he put his hand on his solar plexus.

"Cindy, I know there's something here," Dan said. "I don't know what it is, but it makes me want to cry."

As he reflected on it later, it hit him. He had been transitioning from his career as a wealth planner to someone who helped founders work their way through the exit process of selling their business. Dan had joined a study group that was designed to teach them how to teach others to go through an exit. But the group was rigid, and Cindy's question helped him realize he was working too hard to implement the specific guidelines. The process he was attempting to implement was forced and over-contrived, and it disconnected him from his clients. They were losing trust, and, as Dan discovered, so was he.

In an instant, he knew that he didn't need the group. He needed to trust himself.

That epiphany came with the help of true coaching. Cindy didn't tell Dan what he should or shouldn't do. She asked him a question! The question went to the heart of his problem, and his subconscious knew it. As Dan thought about it, he realized that he had abandoned what he knew to be true about exit and succession planning. It is not a transaction but a discovery process requiring facilitation expertise and project management skills for the bevy of experts needed throughout the life cycle of the business—and especially when moving through a succession and sales transaction. Dan was helping somebody in a high-stakes transaction that involves their life's work. There's a lot of anxiety, complexity, and unfamiliarity. In his haste to find solutions, he had bought a Trojan Horse instead of trusting himself to create a viable process.

The irony? What Dan experienced with Cindy is what his clients needed from him! They needed somebody who could help them get what they wanted without telling them what to do.

Coaching at its best is designed precisely to create this scenario.

That experience changed Dan—both in that moment and in the trajectory of his professional life. He became a student and a fan of that style of leadership coaching. He started reading the literature and attending courses to both improve his receptiveness to coaching and learn how to do it for himself within his own organization. Dan initially didn't have any interest in becoming a professional coach—he was running a successful wealth planning organization and had recently started the Exit Planning Exchange. Most of his clients were business owners, and he was the founder and CEO of two organizations. He had two time-consuming roles: Finding and retaining clients and running a highly engaged board.

To Dan's delight and surprise, his new-found coaching interest changed the way he related to his clients and constituents, and they to him. He became far more effective and satisfied with his professional and employee relationships. Coaching taught Dan to listen better: to show up less judgmental, more open, and more curious. Others, in turn, felt seen and heard—and they trusted him more quickly. He learned that his coaching skills made him better, and not just professionally but in all the roles in his life.

A few years later, an unexpected opportunity led Dan to turn leadership coaching into his profession. A colleague he met through the Exit Planning Exchange asked him if he would be interested in chairing a Vistage peer group. Vistage is a peer mentoring organization for CEOs of small and mid-sized companies that has been around since the 1950s. More than 25,000 CEOs participate every year in a peer group led by experienced business coaches in their area.

Dan was at first skeptical, but he asked a few clients who participated in it, and he was immediately hooked. Coaching became his passion, and working with CEOs in the nexus between leadership and coaching captured his full-time attention. For nearly 8 years he has facilitated a group of 20 high performing CEOs in an all day executive session.

June's story and skill set not only make her supremely qualified as a coach, but also an ideal co-pilot on this journey. As a young child, she had to take a lot of responsibility at home to help take care of her younger siblings when her mother experienced some health setbacks and was in and out of the hospital. When she describes helping her youngest brother manage his anxiety about visiting their mother in the hospital—by reframing the conversation around the elements they could control, like scheduling time at a playground near the hospital before the visit to burn off energy before having to go in and be quiet and still—we can see the thread of that compassion and attention to what others are not only doing and thinking but also feeling in our work today.

That perceptiveness, emotional intelligence and attention to detail helped June go on to have an impressively multi-faceted corporate career—risk management, IT, leading and teaching on diversity, equity and inclusion, accounting, finance, and portfolio analytics. Her work naturally flowed into focusing on asking the most insightful questions vs. being the ultimate subject matter expert for her various reports. Those questions helped her teams move forward, and she became known as a developer of talent.

A coach.

Now, she helps develop senior leaders and their teams in the art and science of leadership and coaching with a keen insight.

As a corporate leader, I was known as a developer of key talent. I had built one of the most diverse teams in our entire organization, and had a wide-ranging set of responsibilities for the organization - from finance to operational risk management to portfolio analytics to file rooms. Despite the breadth of work, I had started to get bored, so I talked my way into a year-long internal leadership development program.

One of the program requirements was to participate in a 4-day diversity & inclusion workshop, designed to raise self-awareness and effectiveness when working across differences. I thought I was very effective already, yet walked into a couple very painful blind spots on Day 2.

During a lunch break on the 3rd day, one of the facilitators took me aside for a 1:1 conversation. She asked me some brilliant, self-reflective questions that helped me move from stuck, shamed and fearful (my own internal narratives) to curiosity, self-compassion and a commitment to do more. She helped me re-write my story, and I created a vision of me facilitating similar workshops for leaders in the future. That was my first memory of truly being coached.

Within 3 years, I left my COO role and became a senior strategy consultant in HR focused on driving greater diversity & inclusion outcomes for a large part of the company, and leading those very same diversity & inclusion workshops for leaders. I knew that creating the changes I was envisioning meant getting the executive team more fully on board, and past their own blind spots and fears. They were going to need more than workshops to get there. I pursued developing my coaching skills with purpose and commitment, as another critical tool in my toolbox to grow leaders. Adding coaching to the mix of strategy and leadership changed everything, and we exceeded all expectations, creating one of the most empowered and high performing work cultures I have ever experienced. From there, I moved into executive coaching, and I've never looked back.

Our combined origin story started in Boston, where we first met briefly at a coaching course in 2016. Two years later, June was helping run a leadership program I joined as a participant. After the session we reconnected and I gave her some of the broad details about the individual clients I was helping in the entrepreneurial space. I was interested in figuring out how to create an external coaching program that would gain traction in the corporate space—right in June's wheelhouse—and she became a trusted coach for me on how to ideate that dream.

But at the same time, June was approaching her 30th year in corporate life and beginning to think about what an entrepreneurial step of her own would look like. We became peer coaches for each other—me coaching her on the move into the entrepreneurial space, and June coaching me on how to make my individual coaching business programmatic. The more we worked together as coachees and coaches, the more it became clear that we had complementary skills that would come together very well as business partners. We actually had to "break" the coach-coachee relationship to have the conversation that would be the genesis of what you're reading–and our clients are experiencing today–to decide to work together. Dan brought his big ideas about how to change leadership, and June worked to craft those ideas into concrete, actionable course material—putting the program together brick by brick.

Our styles and personalities are very different, but also very complementary. For us, tension and friction are something we have learned to embrace as where the real "juice" of progress lies. Those feelings and experiences are grist in the coachee's mill, and are a necessary part of the process of self-organization. June is an expert at guiding experiences so that a coachee can access those potentially unsettling feelings and emotions in a safe, productive way. The best way to describe it is the way an elite race car driver takes apart a track. He or she gets the car right to the edge of the performance envelope to get the fastest lap time, but doesn't go over the edge and lose control of the car—because making massive corrections (or crashing!) defeats the purpose! With June, I feel more free to be honest and open with my passion and creativity. Her steady and strong presence creates a sturdy container that grounds me, helping to avoid overwhelming or confusing the client. On the other side of the ledger, Dan's willingness to be open and bold, to challenge himself and others including June, has helped push us forward creatively and productively.

We believe our collaboration is one of the highest, best examples of trusting the process. As we moved through the complexity of creating something new together for the first time, we persevered and eventually found our rhythm—differentiated skills and experience coming together to form a collective whole that's greater than the sum of its individual parts. And we're both so excited to bring those varied experiences and shared philosophy to this project with the unified voice you're going to hear for the rest of this book.

What makes this the "right" way?

There are plenty of great resources out there about how to improve the ground-level tactics of business. And there's an incredible array of training and technologies to support the ability to sort piles of noisy information.

Power to Coach™ isn't designed to be a replacement for any of those resources.

What we do at MindfulCEO™ is help leaders find the internal elements that build and sustain passion and a sense of meaning around what they do. It's too simple to say that we're helping clients expand the definition of what "success" is for them. It's more accurate to say that we're leading the conversation about what a more complete definition would look like—and how that definition is, by definition, very personal to you, better for your business, and better for the world.

June and Dan's voices are the two main ones you'll hear in this book. Dan has been doing one-on-one and group leadership coaching for a decade, and his clients include some of the most influential and successful executives in technology, media and finance. Dan will be drawing from his experiences in more than 6,000 individual hours of one-on-one executive coaching—along with the skills he developed in his previous careers. June has more than 25 years of experience in executive development both for Fortune 500 companies like Wells Fargo and through her own Tango Leadership consultancy.

Together, we work with individual clients and conduct long-range group leadership development cohorts through MindfulCEO and her company, Tango Leadership. The programs are designed to be a guided cohort experience where CEOs and other leaders can both receive coaching and hone their skills to coach others.

The rich experiences from both individual coaching and the cohorts form the case study backbone of Power to Coach. Your story and your journey is your own, but you'll be able to see parallels in the case studies that provide a frame for the conversation. We'll also share personal stories about our own journeys, and how the trips we've taken have inspired us.

HOW WILL WE WORK TOGETHER?

Adapted from the work of The Leadership Circle

To this end, we'll take you through this journey with our framework for coaching emergent leadership, which we call Theory B - where B stands for belonging.

belonging
/bəˈlôNGiNG,bəˈläNGiNG/
noun

an affinity for a place or situation.
"we feel a real **sense of belonging**"

We'll take you through the five intentional steps that will accelerate your ability to embrace chaos and complexity as the source of growth and innovation as we self-organize, and serve as rich context for your coaching work with leaders around you. The five steps serve as the names and organizing principles behind each chapter, and create the roadmap for where we're going together.

The leaders we coach are often highly accomplished, frequently educated at the best schools in the world, often with advanced degrees. They are smart, well intended, of high character, and with minds that are fine-tuned by their educational experiences. Helping leaders to increase their effectiveness by helping them grow their intellectual abilities does not make sense in this setting. Let's take it a step further. Generally speaking, helping them become intellectually smarter makes about as much sense as helping them to become richer. Both of those assumptions are misguided. We help our clients to be more effective, which means a central focus on relationship management that starts with self-mastery.

Generally speaking, the most potential usually lies in the untapped "intelligence" beyond and below the cranium—in the whole body. This may be easier to understand when you realize our entire nervous system is a much more accurate depiction of what we think of as the brain. Our central nervous system runs throughout the body, even to the outer layer of our skin. Both the stomach and the heart are considered to have their own brains because they send more signals up to the brain than they receive from the brain. To get the full benefit of our inherent human intelligence, we should focus our inquiries on "What am I / are you experiencing?" rather than "What do I/you think?" We help our clients to be fully aware and awake by learning to modulate their entire state of being.

For these reasons, we decided to name the chapters after optimal and mindful states of being with the belief that if the world is changing so should the antiquated approach to leadership.

- **Merge: Resting in Belonging**. In Chapter 2, we start the journey by remembering and noticing our natural state of "merged belonging" as a means of standing in the strength of our interconnected relationships. In our fast-paced and chaotic world, it is easy to escape into ourselves and away from the rest of the world only to find a lonely and isolated place, when what we really need to blossom are healthy relationships with others. When we stop to notice and accept the joining of our inner and outer worlds, we will naturally sense the awe of our coherent and "merged" existence, which is the place of exquisite performance, and a leader's dream! We'll explore how, when we are coaching, we help them to observe what occupies them, and begin to expand and redirect their attention to help them find belonging and meaning in whatever endeavors they choose to pursue.
- **Move: From Chaos to Clarity**. In Chapter 3, we explore how to trigger growth and engagement of the team as we learn how to quiet the noise and find the signal of peak performance. Feel the movement? In this context, coaching is an empowered response to our accelerating world and a perfect complement to effective modern leadership because it helps to forward the action as a healthy and adaptive response to the new complexity we continually face.
- **Trust: Nurturing the Space Within**. In Chapter

4, we learn the importance of self trust, especially as the teams we play on are quickly acquiring new capacities to deal with new challenges. It is how we stay the course and keep our balance in the face of changing conditions. As we hold the balance, agency begins to mount and we discover that it is up to us to stay the course and allow the optimal conditions to cohere in our midst. When coaching, you help leaders lean into their personal growth by grounding them in the power of choice and honing the skill of continuous improvement, especially in an environment of rapidly increasing complexity.

• **Choose: Building the Bridge**. In Chapter 5, we go from stimulus to action in rapid succession by noticing, shaping, choosing, and creating our desired outcomes to best serve ourselves and the systems (e.g. teams and groups) that make up our world. We learn to help our coachees become coachable - open and awake—with the right questions to build their skill of self-architecting and fully appropriating their own vision for peak performance. As this is happening, both the individual and the teams they serve start to differentiate, integrate, and self-organize into more effective cohorts.

• **Integrate: Bringing it All Together**. In Chapter 6, we examine how integration is at the core of our connected reality and the best definition of organizational health. The more tightly integrated we are, the healthier we are. As a collective, we perform at our best, staying present to what is necessary to preserve sustainable whole health in our interconnected environments—which holds true not just for the organization, but the individual lives that collectively animate the business. As a coach, you are able to discern when coaching is the best approach, and coach in the moment without attachment to specific outcomes other than to be in service of your coachee and the teams he or she serves.

At the end of each chapter, we will have a short study guide that summarizes the key points of that chapter, and offers questions for you to consider.

Let's get started.

CHAPTER 1 STUDY GUIDE

Executive Summary:

- Leaders choose to take responsibility for creating their world, and anyone can choose to be a leader.
- Leadership is multidimensional, and demands agility to operate from various aspects of leadership.
- Leaders who coach are the future of business.
- Coaching is a special relationship that helps others discover and get what they want through change, adaptation, and growth. It is designed to help people uncover their internal motivation and inspiration to change, and to develop the skills and behaviors that improve confidence, competence, and ultimately performance.
- Our framework for coaching emergent leadership, which we call Theory B, is anchored in the reality that all humans are interconnected, and it is through relationship to the whole that we experience and accept true belonging.
- Belonging is vital to thriving workplaces and society.
- Emergence is inseparable from the concept of synergy–when the whole is greater than the sum of the parts.
- Great leaders grow more leaders.
- Our intention is to expand your capacity as a leader to hold self, others and the context all at once, and to surf the emergent wave through chaos to complexity and ultimately to self-organization.

Reflection Questions (consider writing your answers in a journal):

- Which of the key points we made surprised you?

- Which were familiar or resonated for you?
- What does leadership mean to you? Who do you choose to be? What is your Work?
- What does belonging mean to you?
- What has been your past experience with coaching?
- What was your key insight or take-away from this chapter?
- What questions are you eager to have answered?

Coaching Questions:

- What is your definition and understanding of coaching?
- What will leveraging the skill of coaching offer you as a leader?
- How can I more actively listen as a leader and a coach?
- What will enhance my ability to question more powerfully as a leader and a coach?
- What do you expect/desire to experience from coaching?

Chapter 2: Merge: Resting in Belonging

"Do not be satisfied with the stories that come before you. Unfold your own myth."

Rumi

Patrick had lots of time, and he had lots of data.

His medical technology company in Boston had been around since the 1980s, and gone through exponential growth leading up to the pandemic—to more than 1,000 employees— and even the shutdowns that came in 2020 hadn't done anything to slow the momentum. The only issue was a seeming dichotomy between the performance of some teams relative to others. Patrick's job as COO was to keep the train running on time. But like the rest of the team, he was working remotely—which made it harder to keep track of the team's day-to-day temperature.

When our coaching call started it was clear that Pat was agitated. When I asked him what was going on, he hesitated and fidgeted as he recounted a series of performance metrics. Some of his teams were performing better in the chaos, while others were slipping and appeared to be lost. Pat was struggling to make sense of the disparity and it was making him uncomfortable.

"I'm noticing the gap widening, too," he said. "A third of the teams are accelerating their growth, while the remaining two thirds are trailing behind their two-year rolling average performance. Their utilization rate is dropping. I just don't understand what is happening."

His confusion was palpable.

"The leaders on the strong teams are more engaged, and they go the extra step to set up bonding activities outside of work—like hiking or playing golf," Patrick said. "Those leaders are curating the team experience—posting photos, keeping engaged in the email threads."

"How is that different from what the underperforming groups are doing?" I asked.

"The other groups," he said, "were laser-focused on metrics—utilization rate, workflow and the other KPIs that made up a lot of the organizational scorecard. They were worried and unhappy."

"You mean the metrics you quoted to me at the start of this call?" I asked.

Patrick paused. "Yes."

Perhaps you have chosen to read this book because you know there's a different way to do things. Perhaps you intuitively understand that long-term, sustainable performance no longer comes from a top-down culture, but from a more distributed and agile culture that is relationally focused. Teams don't do well because managers insist they meet metrics. They do well because leaders liberate them to individually combine their strengths, focusing on the facets of the team goal that they can impact most profoundly.

Good leaders help their teams to cut through the noise to find flow and high performance.

What Patrick's highest performing teams had stumbled upon was the power of personal, relational connections. The conversations those leaders had with their team members focused on the relationships—the wants and needs of team members—the work, and all that was engaging and special about it. That meant that the members of the team were sustained by a true sense of mission and belonging. COVID presented a once-in-a-lifetime disruption to the day-to-day. The high-performing teams were more comfortable with the new normal; they were ok with the disruption and even embraced it, creating new systems that streamlined old processes.

They were rolling with their new circumstances.

New hires commented that they had never felt more integrated than they had during this "remote" experience, because the high-performing leaders had worked so hard to promote the connective tissue between workers who were no longer sitting next to each other in a room as they worked.

To be sure, the high-performing leaders had challenges. Many of them talked about how exhausting it was to take on the extra duty of creating this connective tissue. To suddenly be thrust into a remote work model was at first traumatic. It was chaos that required time and focus to become manageable. Eventually, the strong leaders found the signal in the personal relationships and started moving quickly and having fun in spite of the remote setting. It was a tremendous amount of work, and a great accomplishment.

They had made the new normal "organic." They created and maintained a sense of belonging.

And the teams that had lagged behind?

In those teams, the leaders had fallen victim to a very real phenomenon in our modern world of overwhelming 24-7 information stimulation. The world is a noisy, dense, even suffocating place. It constantly screams for our attention—whether or not it deserves it! The normal, human reaction to this constant barrage is to find it stressful, recoil from it and to search for cover. They were becoming islands unto themselves.

Those other leaders built protective cocoons around themselves and their teams. Head down and just focus on the numbers, they said. The world is a scary place, they believed, so we need to consolidate and think about the fundamentals.

It's understandable. Natural, even.

Humans certainly haven't evolved fast enough to process the amount of information bombarding us every day. In evolutionary terms, the time between frontier folk shooting an animal with bow and arrow so they could cook it over a fire and us ordering sushi and having it delivered is less than a blink.

If we allow it, we're presented with thousands of decisions every day, from scrolling through social media on our phones to answering emails to sending text messages to interacting with people at home and on video meetings to making childcare, financial, social, and healthcare decisions.

The signal—that pocket of high performance and comfort—is in this vast and endless field of stimulus and information.

There's obviously a big difference between getting angry about something you read on Twitter and firing off a response and taking time to make an appointment with the dermatologist because you're concerned about a spot you noticed on your skin. Just as there's a difference between seeing a beautiful picture of a friend's trip to France on Facebook and immersing yourself in your own trip with your family.

And that's just it.

We generally do a particularly bad job sorting through noise to find the signal. For most of us, this effort to keep our heads above the water is subconscious.

We mistake loudness and urgency for importance.

We're wired for pain avoidance, so we often make decisions that relieve short term discomfort but have long-term negative consequences.

We have emotions, and those emotions often provoke responses that consideration and logic might not otherwise support.

That's why coaching—and the culture surrounding coaching—is so relevant right now.

Mindful leadership and the tools that go with it are a way through the noise.

In our practices, we work with clients to help them learn how to become aware of what is happening in the moment both internally and in their environment. As they develop this skill, they start to notice how little time they have historically set aside to pause, reflect and process information. Their decision-making had become reactive—tactical instead of strategic and relentlessly habitual.

This new awareness leads to a calm, mindful presence and presents us with choice – something that prior to gaining this intentional awareness in and amongst the noise we were incapable of noticing. Now we can choose connectedness to others that gives life and work a deeper sense of purpose and meaning.

One client had been working 18 hours a day, seven days a week for months. He had lost key members of his team and when presented with the choice between burdening his already short-handed staff with extra work or taking it on himself, he took the load. So he was performing the role of three different managers, all while trying to find a new chief revenue officer and chief finance officer for his company.

Just looking at Christian's calendar would give even a busy person hives. He spent an average of 12 hours per day in meetings with clients and potential investors, and another three working with his team. And that was before even getting to things like email, industry study and administrative work.

With so much on his plate, every problem seemed like a crisis that required triage. His multi-tasking was burning him out, and it was burning his team out, too.

To help Christian slow down and learn how to quiet the noise, we built a rating system for every piece of news and information that came his way. He made his own version of a war room, with sticky notes he could move around to different priority levels. Through that process, he started to identify core information patterns and how to link them to the company's most important priorities— and he was able to move the non-critical items to the side. He found a system to sort and organize the noise.

Finding the signal in this way is precisely what the most effective performers in any genre do. They sort out the noise and then cancel it by focusing on what is relevant and necessary. To be able to sort out and cancel, we must first notice it and then accept it for what it is. As we do so with the intention of finding the signal, we are learning to be calm and OK with whatever is happening.

We call this Merging with the Field.

In the performance game, this is the skill of skills. And, yes, it is something you can learn—and master.

Coaching (and specifically the notice-pause-reflect-THEN-choose aspect of it) is the active ingredient.

Applied appropriately in leadership development, coaching helps us to see ourselves more clearly, and also see our circumstances more clearly.

You don't get one without the other.

It brings us into a flow state—the state where you feel at peace and one with what is happening. The signal is the clear choice that literally merges us more completely with our environment—whether that's a team in a meeting room, a family in a car headed to vacation or with a loved one taking in a mountain vista.

Kelly Slater is the most decorated surfer of all time. An 11-time world champion, he was competitive into his late 40s against surfers half his age. In a Sports Illustrated article, he articulated what we're talking about here:

Slater, one of the all time great surfers, remembers a trick an old friend taught him: Laugh at the waves. "Get rid of the fear," he says. "Understand what the wave is going to do. And become part of it." That was the way. Become part of it. And he found that to do that, to know the ocean, he had to know himself. "You're dealing with a lot of unknowns," he says. "But there is a pattern in the ocean. Yes, there is some kind of luck—but it just seems like the more connected you are with yourself, the better luck you have."

The term "trick" is so important in that passage.

Why?

Because Slater learned a singular technique to do what he needed to do. It wasn't an arduous process that required tremendous willpower. It was more about accepting something as omnipresent as gravity. "Merging" in this way isn't about doing something new, but about opening up and allowing yourself to experience what's really happening.

And what *is* really happening?

Our persistent reality is that we're all interconnected into a web of life. Even if you don't feel particularly *integrated* with those around you, you are! We need each other to propagate life. We merge together to form communities, businesses, teams—you name it. Thousands of years of evolution have programmed us to crave connections. To search for belonging. How many times have you heard somebody say, "I want to be a part of something bigger than myself?" With meaning and purpose, we gain the power to form and keep sustainable relationships and enjoy a richness of life that goes beyond dollars in an account or numbers on a spreadsheet.

What does the opposite look like?

Feeling separated or disconnected is endemic in modern culture, unfortunately. Dan Siegel, a professor of psychiatry at the University of California and author of *Interconnected*, calls this renegade incarnation of "separate self" a cancer or autoimmune disease that presents an existential threat to our species. Why cancer? When cancer cells form in the body, they're an out-of-control growth of one type of cell that is harmful to the system as a whole. When our mental construction of "separate self" gets out of control, it can be analogous to a cancer of modern society. Our wants and behaviors run amok and go out of sync with the larger system of the whole.

The antidote to this?

Integration. Siegel calls integration "optimal health," and uses the acronym FACES to describe the healthy systems it represents: Flexible, Adaptive, Coherent, Energized and Strong.

The implications for coaching are enormous.

What is coaching, fundamentally?

It's about helping people align with the emergent process of life. To stay with and lean into what's coming— and to learn how to coach and develop those around you.

You can dismiss these concepts as self-help mumbo-jumbo, or you can do what elite leaders and performers do and make some space between what you experience and your reaction to it, and thereby choose to think in a different way.

What if you could develop a curious, non-judgmental mind?

What if you could see yourself more clearly, and also see others and the world around you more clearly?

What if you could slow down enough to see what's here, right now?

Wouldn't that deeper connection to self and to others make you a better leader? A better friend? A better parent? A better partner? A better coach?

We realize that sounds ambitious, but in experience as both a coach and a person being coached, we have seen how these skills transform a person's ability to sort through the chaos, learn from it and find an optimal response.

Think about what's at stake here. The top-down, data-driven management style that has been the operating system for the better part of 70 years is unsustainable. In general terms, it turns up the heat. You know this or you wouldn't be looking for a different approach.

With better tools and a different outlook, you can find that sense of purpose and meaning—*and* find better performance for yourself and your team. They will sort the data better and find meaning in the grind.

What does this "awareness" look like? We'll describe what it means to us, and you decide if it's something that resonates with you.

For thousands of years, different civilizations have practiced the art of meditation—channeling more "awareness" of what is going on in the "field" that surrounds us. The term "meditation" might conjure some negative associations for you, but we're merely using the term to describe the act of quieting your mind so you can train your perception on the world around you.

Philosophers, artists, scientists—and, more recently, athletes—have all examined and used this concept of quietness and noticing to expand into their work. We're sure you've heard about NBA players being "in the zone," where it felt like they couldn't miss. Or, baseball pitchers saying they felt like they were looking down on themselves performing in a crucial moment in the game.

The exact chemical processes going on in the brain during these moments is beyond the scope of this book, but in basic terms, scientists have discovered that this "zone" or "mindful" state is where the most efficient human learning comes from. It's the state that most children are in up until age seven—when, for example, it's so much easier for them to learn how to ski or hit a golf ball than it is for their adult parents! It's also that sense of calm—especially in the midst of what others would experience as hectic and complex is a performance superpower. When it happens in a team, you've really found the ultimate manifestation of meaning, belonging and merging.

How does that compare to the state of awareness you and I are in most of the time day to day? Instead of this soft, panoramic flow state, we're in a constant state of focused triage. A problem or issue pops up, and we train our mental flashlight on it and look for a solution. Like the old Whack-a-Mole game, another thing crops up and we point the flashlight over there and take the next turn.

Make no mistake. The human brain is an amazing miracle. You've probably figured out a way to do this focus-juggling thing well enough to be good at what you do. But operating that way inexorably disconnects you from yourself and from others and explains burn out.

How do you intentionally make this shift back to flow state and away from triage? It's easier than you think.

It starts with tuning into your sense of awe. We'll share a few personal examples with you to help illustrate this point.

A few years ago, June said yes to an opportunity to spend a week off the grid on over 400 acres of wooded lands in northern Minnesota to experience dog sledding with a group of 9 other women. It was mid-February, bitterly cold, and the first few days were spent just learning the ropes - how to harness & handle the dogs, how to ride in the sled, how to manage yourself in a crash and how to read the miles and miles of trails. As you might imagine, there was a tremendous amount to learn about this unfamiliar environment, and the days were both physically demanding and mentally exhausting from the constant state of attention demanded. As we mentioned above, it was 4 days in nearly constant triage - do this - check! - now this - check! - and this ...

On the 5th day, the weather shifted, and so did June. It was a balmy 20 degrees, with bright clear skies and brilliant sunshine flashing off the snow and ice that covered nearly everything. As she stepped out of the cabin to prepare for the first runs of the day, June paused and breathed the air in deeply. She noticed the warmth of the sun on her face, the cracking of branches finally giving in to the weight of the heavy snow, the panting and howling of the dogs in anticipation, and the steady beating of her heart.

As she moved toward the dogs, she had a sense of awe, calm and unconscious competence. She noticed one of the dogs had wrapped his chain around their post. Without conscious thought, she moved into the dog's area, greeted him, managed his jumping while untangling the chain, and moved on toward Akiak. She harnessed her with ease, and navigated her toward the sled, hooking her up and building her excitement at the same time.

On the back trail, hair whipping behind her while mushing for only her second time, June's actions were unconscious and totally in flow - one with the team and the trails as if she had run those trails her whole life. She cried at the beauty of the experience and laughed out loud at the same time as she approached the cabins once more, bringing the sled to a stop.   She had merged with the field, at one with all of the elements of her environment, performing at her peak while losing her sense of time.

Years ago, I made a trip with my wife Ann to the Amalfi Coast, in Italy. We arrived at our villa, which was perched 4,000 feet above the Mediterranean Sea on a spit of rock. The villa was built into the side of the cliff face, which meant that when we approached it from the land side, it looked very modest. We entered the top floor, and as my wife made her way to a small window in front of her, I could see her entire body language change.

It wasn't until the window came into my view that I understood. My brain couldn't make sense of what my eyes were seeing. The sea and sky merged into a uniform cobalt blue, and it was only when I saw the tiny buildings thousands of feet below that I could orient myself.

Ann was crying from the beauty, and I burst into tears, too.

We were experiencing the "field." We weren't examining something as if it were a specimen, but were at one with the environment.

We had merged with the field, and experienced that same sense of belonging I described above.

That deep connection is something I'm sure you've experienced. It could be the rapture of being in a throbbing crowd at a concert from a musician you love. It can happen as you experience art or theater, or when you're competing in a sport. It's also a piece of why romantic love is so powerful. The connection you form with another person can bring you into that state of flow—as can work when we strike the right balance.

Unfortunately, most people only experience this in fleeting moments throughout their lives.

But what if you can make that flow the rule and not the exception?

That's what the culture of coaching is (or should be) designed to do.

Let me give you a concrete example from our practice.

June and I were working with a client named Eddie, who is the founder of a successful venture capital firm. Eddie built his business literally by himself—making all the calls and taking all the risks. But as his firm grew, he needed to add staff so he could scale the business. And that's where the problems started to crop up.

Eddie was *intense*.

He was a brash, aggressive guy, and over time he became more and more aware that something was off. His presence was not having the impact he intended. He began to become curious whether he was too hot for his team to handle productively. With some candid feedback from his wife and a trusted colleague, he decided to seek out an executive coach to help figure out what was happening.

Eddie understood that the qualities that made him successful—fearlessness, aggression—weren't necessarily the ones he needed in the moment to keep growing and connecting. As I asked questions about his approach, he began to notice that he was making his professional (and personal) life more difficult than it had to be.

We began by simply assigning descriptions to his default state. What was he experiencing–emotions and feelings–when these situations occurred? We then began to explore other possible outcomes, and how those might feel. We then compared and contrasted the possible differing felt experiences.

"Which feels better, Eddie?" I asked.

He stood up. Burst out laughing. Looked at me credulously and threw his hands in the air.

"Really? It's that easy?"

"What do you want, Eddie? Make a choice. This is your life to live."

He sat back down, crossed his arms, looked down and went silent.

Eddie was in deep, quiet contemplation. Something very real was at play. Something was shifting. He eventually broke the silence, saying, "Yeah, I'm ready. How do we do this?"

We started by showing Eddie the concrete ways he could intentionally create this shift.

It's something you can do, too.

First, breathe. Take a long, deep breath, filling your chest with as much air as you can. Raise your shoulders as you do it, and then breathe out slowly through your mouth. Let your chest collapse and your shoulders drop, and empty your lungs completely.

Breathe in for a count of six, hold for a count of three, then breathe out for a count of six and hold for a count of three.

Do this circuit three times, then resume your normal breathing pattern.

Now, work on your intense focus. Pick up any object near you. Feel it carefully with your fingertips, and notice its detail. What does it feel like? What is its temperature and texture? Does it have a smell or a taste? What is something you notice about it that you hadn't noticed before?

Do this study for two minutes, exploring this object as if it is new to you. Think about what it could be used for in ways other than its intended use. You can even think of a new name for it!

Put the object down and gently put your fingertips together and rub them gently enough that you can feel the ridges. Focus on this sensation for 60 seconds.

Now, pause and take a deep breath. Close your eyes and listen for the sounds around you. Which ones are the farthest away? Which are the closest? Can you hear your own breathing, or your heart beating?

Return to normal listening and breathing, open your eyes and move on with your day.

When you take control of your state this way, you've just found a leadership superpower.

Once Eddie learned how to make the shift, he needed to understand where he was shifting from—and what he was shifting to. It starts by learning how to take a "body snapshot" of where you are in any given moment, and attach descriptors to it.

Freeze in place. What position are you in? What do you notice about your shoulders? Are they tight? What about your face? What does this posture feel like? What emotions and energy are there?

Now, ask yourself: What other choices are there?

What does "confident" look like? Head up? Shoulders square? Feet firmly on the floor?

How about "compassionate?" Shoulders softer? Eyes wide? Arms and chest open?

"Curious?" Leaning in? Smiling? Hands open to take hold of something new?

Now reflect. What posture will give the best energy for what the moment requires? What choice do you make? Once you do, then act. Move into that posture and do and say from there.

The net?

It took time and courage and patience, but Eddie and his team eventually began to find their mojo. It was not a perfectly clean and linear process. Eddie was coming to a new truce with himself and essentially creating new trust and relationships with his teams. Several of the relationships were too damaged to repair. But three years later, Eddie was in one of our Power to Coach Programs learning how to use coaching skills to become a more effective CEO. He was primed to learn how to help others accomplish what he had—consciously making choices that will change their lives and accelerate their performance and joy in their work.

Veronica's story is a similar one. She was the new chief marketing officer for her firm, and her team was going through its fourth major restructure in the last 12 months. It was easy to see how it was wearing on her. As she and June talked, her shoulders were slumped, her chin was down and she kept looking to the side as she talked.

"I feel defeated," she said. "I can't help my people. They're struggling with all this change and feeling powerless."

She went on to say that she had been in their shoes a few months before, wondering if she had what it took to make it through the next round of reorganization.

"What are you noticing about how you're sitting right now?"

"Well, I'm kind of hunched over," she said.

"How easy is it for you to breathe?"

She immediately registered that her breathing was really shallow. She stood up and did the breathing exercise we just described, and the coaching session concluded.

A week later, Veronica came into the next session very excited.

"I noticed my posture was so bad during meetings, so I bought a stand-up desk," she said. "The team is noticing a different energy, and there's excitement about the new direction. I challenged the new CEO to make good on a strategic investment in marketing. I'm using this new fuel, and it feels great."

What Eddie and Veronica learned to practice was mindfulness. It's become a catchy term in leadership circles, but it's actually a veteran with thousands of years of experience in religions like Buddhism.

Mindfulness is a process that brings us into the present moment, to merge with the now. It lets you ground yourself, take stock in what you see, feel and experience, and reacquaint yourself with the resources and information at hand.

So much of the attention we place in modern life is like a flashlight. The sound goes off on your smartphone, and you reflexively pick it up and stare at the notification. You get an email from somebody with a problem they need you to solve and you drop everything to bore down on it. We jump from fire to fire, task to task, call to call, so much so that the bigger story is often obscured.

Mindfulness is a process that brings us into the present moment.

But with mindfulness practice, you can turn all of this attention to more of a "lantern" type. The landscape is illuminated, and you can see things in context. By simply learning to take a moment and reconnect when you're feeling anxious and stressed, like Eddie and Veronica did, you're using a powerful balancing tool that is always at your disposal.

As we discussed earlier, the surfing metaphor is a powerful one for what this journey looks like.

The ocean is the field of possibilities, and the wave is just one of the many powerful emergent qualities of the ocean. The surfer looks for his or her moment and place of highest potential.

The wave in the metaphor can symbolize many things, even our life. It could be our career, our family, our team. The most salient point of the metaphor is that we must participate with nature and what is happening in our midst, rather than compete with it.

I experienced this first-hand.

My father was an extraordinary man. He was not flawless. His father was the oldest child of an immigrant family from Calabria, Italy, and his mother was an immigrant from Los Mochis, Mexico. They struggled, and succeeded. The struggle made my father view his world as hostile and helped shape him into an intense and wildly ambitious man. That he was smart and handsome were bonuses that helped him make a hostile truce with the world on his way to becoming a successful businessman.

I am my father's son, and I naturally adopted his perspective on life—and was also wildly aggressive and intense. I was on a mission to shape the world to my will. I learned—after years of struggle—the universe always wins!

That's when I began to learn to surf the waves of life.

When I did, doors and opportunities began to open for me. I began to realize that life was hostile only because that was my perspective and my belief.

My context was skewed.

Now I know, from personal experience, that as soon as I believe what I think, it becomes my reality. I believed that life was hostile and I had to subdue it and drag it in the direction that I wanted. When I did that, life was hostile in return. It was truly tiring and burnout was my constant companion.

Life changed when I realized that I could shape my life as I shifted my perspective to see a universe of possibilities. I began to understand and merge with the power of its waves.

The "field" is what it is. It could be a villa in the Italian Riviera, or it could be a conference room in Camden, New Jersey. The waves are what they are. They don't care if you're tall or short, Ivy League educated or a high school dropout, super fit or more comfortable on the couch.

You can decide to experience the wave by surfing it and channeling its power into speed and exhilaration. Or you can try to fight it. To impose rules and order upon it. Or you can just passively lay on your board and let the waves carry you where they will.

Which way do you think will help you perform your best? Which way will be more productive in your role as a coach for others? Instead of looking for strength, grit and leverage, what if you looked for synchrony, resonance and harmony around you?

What if you choose which wave you wanted to catch? What if you were determined to merge with the wave? To merge with the field?

What sets leaders apart now? We argue that it isn't being able to crunch the data, formidable technical knowledge or calculated ruthlessness. It is understanding humans. Compassion. Being connected to the people on their teams and to the world around them—and being at peace when the big waves are coming to shore.

At the risk of "over-metaphoring" you, you can think of the process of developing yourself as a leader or as a coach as similar to that of a stem cell. Within the body, stem cells are almost magic. They can morph into whatever kind of cell the body needs at the time—from bone to cartilage to brain matter to connective tissue. What is that stem cell doing but taking its cues from the environment around it and transforming itself into what is the highest and best service for the overall system?

In our view, finding harmony with that natural system is written into our DNA.

Great leaders see themselves and see the environment around them. They're searching for the optimal state-of-being by noticing what is happening in the moment. Like the stem cell, they're responding to the field to find the signal so it becomes what it must.

How can you develop this skill in yourself?

Through coaching.

How can you build a team around you that can multiply that effect through the ranks of your team?

Through coaching.

When you walk into a meeting, what does the "field" look like for you? Are you focused on what you're about to say, or are you scanning the room trying to ascertain its energy?

What does the chatter around the table tell you?

Who around the table is present, and who is distracted?

What are the groups, and who seems to be isolated?

What does the overall body language look like? Is it a confident, assured group? Are they nervous? Angry?

What are the outside factors in the organization or in the world that could be changing the energy in the room?

Once you notice those things, how do you decide what state of mind you need to be in to bring the room what it needs?

To build your best team and best organization, how do you coach others to learn how to tune in in these particular ways?

That's the Power to Coach.

What did that look like for Patrick?

I asked him what success would look like now that he understood the difference between the two groups of teams—and what the challenges were going forward for the leaders of both.

How would he transplant some of the connective tissue from the thriving teams, while also building a culture that would take some of the responsibility and weight off the shoulders of the successful leaders?

He decided to put to paper what the specific communication strategies the successful teams were using, and use storytelling organization-wide to establish those strategies as part of the culture. They would become the structure for the entire organization to embrace and enforce, not just for those few leaders to drag through in their personal time.

Patrick decided to repeatedly reinforce that producing quality work was his most important metric— not dry KPIs like "utilization rate." And when discussing how the business was doing, the language would always be framed around the achievements of people in their roles, not numbers on a financial affidavit.

Veronica's team is thriving, and so is the organization. She coached two of her direct reports (and former peers) into finding roles as CMOs at other organizations, helping them follow their passions. They in turn helped her successfully backfill the openings their departures created. There was no need for lay-offs, as shuffling the seats created all the space that was needed for everyone to grow.

Connection.

Let's learn more about how to build that.

FRAMEWORK: MERGE: RESTING IN BELONGING

"Merge" in its definitive sense means to combine, unite, or coalesce. Why is this such an important concept to understand, accept and embrace? Because—whether you accept it or not—humans do not exist in a vacuum. Even the most hard-core independent entrepreneur needs a market, and by definition, a market is a combination of people or entities that come together to determine value. Unless you decide you're going to live as a hermit on an island somewhere with no electricity, internet, professionally-made tools, or contact with the rest of the world, you're going to have to contend with some number of the rest of us to get on.

Great leaders know that helping to provide the context around complex, stressful situations—to develop and illuminate the pathways toward belonging and teamwork—is a massive competitive advantage. We're all hard-wired to read and respond to the immediate threats around us: You can thank thousands of years of evolution and the on-the-job training that makes our blood pressure spike, cortisol flow, and senses get heightened when there are real or perceived local threats. The power of merging comes by being able to intersperse those real and valuable tactical "sprints" with a more strategic overhead view. In that view, we can take a breath and stay connected to the bigger purpose, and see that we in fact have what we need around us. That feeling of connectedness and belonging is one of the fundamentals of the human experience.

What does this look like when it's working in its ideal iteration? You're at peace with yourself and at peace with the world around you. Your internal and external world are moving like two lanes of traffic coming together into one high-speed flow on the expressway, so to speak. We call it the "ecosystem of you"—a collection of varied but integrated parts that make a whole that's greater than the sum of its parts. National Geographic describes it perfectly: A "bubble of life," where living organisms join the landscape and weather to form a sustaining, ever-recharging cycle. In human terms, Archbishop Desmond Tutu described it—a concept Africans call Ubuntu—powerfully: "It's the essence of being human. It is part of the gift that Africa is going to give the world. It embraces hospitality, caring about others, being willing to go the extra mile for the sake of another. We believe that a person is a person through other persons—that my humanity is caught up and bound up in yours... The solitary human being is a contradiction in terms, and therefore you seek to work for the common good because your humanity comes into its own in community. In belonging."

To merge is to rest in belonging. To experience being part of something greater than you or me, which seems to be a universal desire and instinct.

Coaching is fundamentally about helping people to align with the ever-emergent process of life. To stay with and even lean into the process of self-organization and emergence is crucial to growth, performance, and satisfaction. This is where the real meat of peak performance lives—not in the magic of some formula on a consultant's spreadsheet.

In this learning process, we'll be examining many of the conversations and strategies you can be having with yourself and your teams to help encourage and accelerate this self-organizing and emergence:

What is emerging for you?

What's opening up and accelerating for you and your organization?

How are your skills differentiating?

Where do you need to stay, dig in, and remain patient?

What is the quality of your connections?

What's gelling?

What's new in your bubble?

What threatens your bubble?

Conversely, you can decide to fight that reality, like Ayn Rand wrote about in "Atlas Shrugged" and "The Fountainhead." You can promote a Darwinian survival-of-the-fittest culture that encourages individual aggression and fetishizes winning at all costs.

In natural history, that's what happened when a small group of hunters backed by financiers and traders in the American East came out and killed millions of bison in just a few years for their hides. When the American bison were eradicated from the Western prairies, those lands lost the keystone that sustained the ecosystem. The enormous herds walked the land eating the prairie grasses, spreading seed and fertilizer, aerating the soil and also providing native people a supply of meat, fur, and leather. When the seeds could no longer spread as effectively and the native people lost their food supply, thousands of acres of prairie turned to dusty near-desert and tens of thousands of humans lost their way of life.

The large-scale bison hunters were like rogue cells inside the human body that hyperproduce some certain kind of protein that turns into a cancerous tumor that threatens the existence of the entire system. The merchants producing shoes from the bison leather made their fortune while the wasted carcasses of all the bison rotted and the bones bleached in the emerging desert. Two hundred years later, we're still contending with the environmental fallout from the desertification of the middle of the country—and entire cultures were wiped out.

For some shoes.

The challenge for us? Realizing that the power of emergence works just as efficiently and relentlessly in a case like the one that devastated the American bison as it does in a positive, generative case. Like anything else, we can choose to use our powers for "good" or for "evil."

CHAPTER 2 STUDY GUIDE

Executive Summary:

- Energy flows where your attention goes.
- Mindfulness brings us into the present moment.
- Intentionally developing a mindful state raises new awareness that allows you to find the Signal in the Noise.
- Merging with the Field is about opening up to the experience of what's really happening, and creating space between the experience and your reaction.
- Through coaching, you help others observe what occupies them, begin to expand and redirect their attention and help them align with the emergent process of life.

Reflection Questions (consider writing your answers in a journal):

- Which of the key points we made surprised you?
- Which were familiar or resonated for you?
- To what do you tend to pay attention?
- What brings you into the present moment?
- What was your key insight or take-away from this chapter?
- What questions are you eager to have answered?

Coaching Questions:

- What are you noticing?
- What are you feeling right now?
- What is important about this for you?
- What am I learning?
- What do I want to be different?

Chapter 3: Move from Chaos to Clarity—Ride the Emergent Wave

"I used to think that the worst thing in life was to end up alone. It's not. The worst thing in life is to end up with people who make you feel alone."

Robin Williams

Margaret was controlling the chaos—or so she thought.

As the CEO at a dynamic, fast-moving B2B tech company, she wore a lot of hats—from chief growth officer to human resource director to payroll manager. She also had the calendar to match, crammed from 7:30 in the morning to well after dinner with a blizzard of calls, meetings, and rainmaking responsibilities.

The velocity of that schedule meant that she needed an executive assistant that could work proactively in a fast-paced environment. There wasn't time to always be explaining processes or establishing priorities very far down the list.

For years, Lydia had performed well in that executive assistant role. She played a very important part in giving Margaret the support she needed to grow revenue by more than 150 percent over three years. A potential investment from a venture capital firm was on the horizon, which meant the stakes were very high.

Margaret trusted Lydia completely, and their communication styles were a perfect match. The relationship had real warmth and depth to it. Which is why it was so distressing to Margaret when things changed—like so many experienced—at the onset of COVID-related remote work.

When Margaret and Lydia weren't in the same physical space every day, Lydia would seem to disappear. She was wonderful in a crisis—like taking the initiative to save one deal by getting critical documents out to Margaret on the road when Margaret was still in the air with no access to email or phone to request them. But she was falling short on many of the mundane tasks that are the bread-and-butter of an executive assistant, like updating the schedule.

A complicating factor? Because of their warm personal relationship, Margaret knew about Lydia's situation at home. Lydia was a single mother raising two children on her own, and she was frequently exhausted by the effort it took to get the kids everywhere they needed to be in addition to her busy work schedule.

When Margaret came for a coaching session, it was clear she was troubled about something. After some small talk, she went right to the issue with Lydia.

The personal part was painful, but Margaret felt like she was drowning without the support she needed to balance the chaos. She was wondering what she could do to help Lydia improve her performance—or if it was time to make a change.

The coaching session started with a seemingly simple question.

"What do you want from Lydia?"

Margaret answered right away. "I want to know what's going on with her, and why she seems to disappear," she said.

"Well, have you asked her those questions?"

Margaret looked startled.

"Should I? Is that appropriate?"

What followed was a rich exchange, where we examined the landscape around what was fair game to inquire about as both a supervisor and friend—and how to take a breath and take some time to think about what the most productive approach as a coach and leader might be. We helped Margaret learn to carefully distinguish between the tactical issue about Lydia's work rate versus her relationship to—and responsibility for— what was happening. We got to a place where Margaret established that it was valid for her to both express her concern and offer support, <u>and</u> that it was crucial to make it clear to Lydia she cared about her as a friend in addition to getting a clear resolution about the workplace elements that weren't functioning the way they needed to.

Reinforced by the coaching session, Margaret went to Lydia and asked her if there was anything happening that was distracting her from her work, and if there was anything Margaret could do to help.

She learned that Lydia's former husband suffered from severe post-traumatic stress after a deployment in Iraq, and his behavior toward Lydia and their children forced them to relocate several times for their safety. She had learned to live in a constant state of crisis triage, but with the help of a therapist, was slowly gaining a sense of control in her life.

The conversation was somber and deep; it brought the women even closer together, and the compassion that both women felt for each other reinforced their connection.

Trust grew.

Lydia's performance quickly rebounded to an even higher level than it was before remote work started. When Margaret's small staff returned to the office eight months later, they were more than 50 percent above their revenue targets for the year because of how effectively the team was working together. Intentional Change Theory is a body of research dedicated to understanding the mental and emotional scaffolding required to create real and sustained change. Research in that field has shown that passion and desire for change makes the likelihood of that change 60 or 70 percent higher than if the change is motivated by threat or fear. The carrot is indeed more effective in the long term than the stick.

The purpose of this story is not to show you that every instance of poor performance has underlying rationale that should cause a leader to avoid making a change. And it doesn't mean leaders should not be holding team members accountable for their performance. Accountability is the backbone of any healthy relationship, and sometimes changes need to happen for everyone involved.

What we're talking about here is the connective tissue between team members. Between humans. Why are we doing this? Building a bond with the members of your team is an act that resonates. It makes the effort— the journey—worth it. But more than that, it not only is the catalyst for the peak performance so many leaders are trying to extract from their teams, it is also pragmatic. What is the cost—in time and expense—to find, on-board, and retain productive team members? Working with good people through their life's ups and downs can be a redemptive experience that pays lasting dividends and builds healthy cultures.

Instead of treating people like replaceable commodities, connecting with them inspires team members to be connected and committed to their work. Instead of putting the time in out of fear of being replaced if they don't, team members commit energy and effort because they get satisfaction from their contribution to the success of the whole.

If you needed more proof about this concept, COVID certainly provided it in the last few years. Another client, Juan, came to June overworked, burned out, and concerned that he wouldn't be able to rebuild a viable team. In January 2020, he had nearly 200 people working seamlessly to operate two dozen shops inside a large international airport. His people had the highest efficiency and customer satisfaction scores in the industry, and Juan was often tapped to coach leaders from other regions who were struggling.

By May of that year, COVID brought air travel to a standstill. Juan was forced to lay off all but five of his team members. It was a painful, exhausting, chaotic time. And when air travel came roaring back, it didn't get any easier. Many of Juan's previous team members had moved on to other gigs, and it was complicated, time-consuming, and expensive to rebuild his staff. Juan was personally responsible for supply chain management, incorporating new safety procedures, training, payroll—you name it, including working the register when there weren't enough staff to cover.

Could Juan have looked at his situation like a chess player looks at a board, and consider his team members as faceless pieces? That might have been the "easiest" way to do it. But as June worked through their coaching sessions, Juan saw that the path to rebuilding his team was to prioritize bringing in people who shared his commitment and vision, showing his commitment to them and giving them the freedom and authority to take things off his plate. He was intentionally employing a more open and distributed approach to leadership. He started with the most critical jobs—front line workers. He moved in closer to his team, checking in on their mental health and satisfaction. He included them in the idea generation process and gave them a stake in the successful hiring of new team members by rewarding productive referrals.

Juan's team members began training each other and building documentation of those procedures. Instead of operating as a director, Juan was a facilitator. He set the music, got the dancing started and got out of the way—which gave him time to tackle the big-picture issues.

Juan moved from chaos to self-organization. And a new, more agile and integrated team emerged from that chaos. By the end of 2020, Juan's team was operating with even more productivity, internal satisfaction, and customer satisfaction than before COVID.

Stories like these might present a certain kind of challenge to the orthodoxy of "leadership" and "productivity" training many have come to accept as the law of the land. But it's only in the last 125 years or so that we've made the silos of specialization and the commoditization of people our preferred strategy for imposing order on chaos.

But how is that really working for us?

Frank had to re-imagine his role as a leader and how he relates to others. Dan and Frank spent a lot of time mindfully imagining a new reality – literally.

First, I had him relax. To do so, I took him through a deep breathing exercise to get him inducted into a mindful, full body experience. I'd ask him to first imagine prior "generous experiences of helping others to get what they want." I'd ask, once he had the experience in mind, "What is that like? What is the energy in your body?" I then asked him to take a "body snapshot" of the particular energy profile so he could remember it and bring it back when he needed it.

I also asked if a metaphor to describe the sensation came to mind.

He said, "it feels like a spinning top in my belly."

Next, I said, let's now imagine your future, three years out. Imagine yourself somewhere grand, where you are celebrating the last three years, which have far exceeded expectations. I was specific, asking him NOT to project into the future, but rather to imagine himself in the future, looking back.

"Who is there with you, and what has happened?"

We stayed in this mode for some time, pulling out as many details as possible and beginning to enrich his imagined future state. The third time we went through the visualization, months later, I asked him how his imagined relationships were different from those he has today. This question surprised him, but not more than his answer.

At first, he laughed. And then he said, "I am trusting others and they are trusting me."

"How is that different from today?" I asked.

He opened his eyes and looked squarely in mine. His gaze was fixed for what felt to be minutes. When he finally spoke he simply said, "I protect myself, assuming that if I don't, I will get hurt." With that, he dropped his elbows to his knees and his face into his hands, staying there for several minutes.

The real work was about to happen.

First the chaos. Frank now had a "knowing" about what lay ahead. Now he had to start believing in it and practicing with it. This was a new club he had never swung before. Frank was about to be humbled.

We next did a 360-degree interview with all of his senior team to get their candid feedback about their relationship with Frank. The noise got significantly louder. His fears were confirmed, and three of his five leaders left in the next 6 months. To his credit, Frank hung-in, trusting his decisions. He began to acquire new self-care routines that had eluded him all his life.

He began to have some awareness around his diet, he drank less and he began working out a little. He also began to enjoy "slow mornings" that included morning meditation. His first positive feedback came from his family. He and his wife found a family counselor. He had some mending to do there as well.

Before the year was out, the chaos began to quiet - it cooled down a bit but was still complex. He was now having to fix and change things in the business. Two of his five senior leaders were still with him, and pushing for change. It was a good sign that they felt comfortable enough to push on, but there was a lot of organizational work that had to be done, and control that Frank had to learn how to share.

He had entered the phase of re-imagining the business.

Three years later, Frank is a new man, and his business is changing faster than he and his team can keep up. They have officially transitioned into the self-organizing phase of their recovery as things are gelling. Frank is not only trusting others, he is trusting himself more, and he and his team are beginning to experience some big wins again.

Frank *emerged*. He did his work, remaking himself and his world view. He intentionally transformed into a better version of himself. As he did so, he became more valuable to his team as he reconnected more deeply and in a healthier way with his business. His example inspired others, and what emerged was a happier and more productive team that had endured chaos, complexity, and self-organization as it remade itself following Frank's example.

FRAMEWORK: MOVE

The cleanest definition I've heard for the term *emergence* comes from David Pines, the co-founder in residence at the Santa Fe Institute—a research group dedicated to the study of complex systems. Emergence is behavior in a complex, adaptive system that isn't present in its individual parts. The examples in nature are endless–in fact, the main point of this book is that emergence *is* nature, and to conceive of a leadership, management, or coaching system that are at odds with this principle would seem to be a recipe for failure!

What happens when the elements of a system go through emergence? They self-organize to this more "advanced" state. Whether you're talking about water droplets emerging and self-organizing into snowflakes or humans banding together to form tribes, communities, cities, and nations, it's the same phenomenon.

Because systems can be very complex, it might seem like things are happening at random. But look more closely and you see systems within systems, all emerging and self-organizing.

Take the snowflake example.

Snowflakes start as water droplets, and when those droplets cool and freeze into ice crystals, multiple crystals link into snowflakes that are unique from one another, but all made up of specific geometric patterns. No two snowflakes are identical, but no snowflake is cylindrical, or an amorphous blob.

As the droplets freeze into unique, individualized crystals, they merge with other unique crystals to form a fully realized whole—that is also completely unique. If you zoom out to the macro level and think about humans in the same way, it becomes clear how and why chaos theory and self-organization are crucial concepts to lean into.

Think about how prehistoric man figured out how to survive and thrive. The more solitary a human was, the more his existence depended on finding resources right now. If you couldn't figure out a way to find something or kill it, you starved. In the chaos of prehistory—the lack of organized language, the short lifespan, the brutality of the conditions—we figured out how to band together. We figured out how to use our unique skills in specialization to build organized communities. We created languages, stored food, developed cultures—and made art.

Over millennia, our evolutionary story has determined that we need human connection. We thrive on relationships with depth. We need communities not just to survive, but to thrive. There's a greater sense of purpose—a sense of joy—in doing things that matter.

We *move* together as we *move with the signal*.

What does the process of that movement look like? Complexity science–the intersection of physics, probability, computer science, evolutionary biology, neuroscience, and human behavior–has developed a roadmap for us to follow. It starts with chaos, a seemingly random setting of disarray. From chaos we move to complexity–where we begin to gain understanding of the building blocks that make up the whole–we go through what is known as liminal space, or a period of transition. After complexity, there's another movement through liminal space before we accelerate into self-organization behaviors.

It might sound arbitrary to define these phases– and to define the spaces between the phases–but there's a reason for it. The only way to actually move purposefully from chaos to complexity to self-organization–or to lead others on that journey–is to be purposeful about identifying where you are at any given moment. You have to be able to pause, assess, and orient, which is how we find the signal. Once the signal clears, movement is natural and inevitable.

Think about a scenario when you were in chaos. What was productive for you there? Was it blindly acting out, doing *something* vs. doing *nothing*? Or would it have been more productive to begin to ask questions of yourself?

What am I noticing?

What can I accept?

What do I want?

What am I learning?

When you're in chaos, you're the subject. Forces are acting upon you. When you move into liminal space, you're going from being in the subject to being an observer - noticing the shift and the movement. You go from being in it to being a person who sees it in context. It is in the noticing that the liminal space is created as a threshold between the chaos and complexity - or between complexity and self-organizational. To enhance this ability to notice is deeply satisfying, giving one a sense of control because you have identified where you are and where you are heading.

The first shift into complexity puts you in position to say, I understand there are elements to this puzzle. I may not know what they all are, but they are available to be known and understood. This is a massive shift! You're moving around the room and identifying all the pieces of furniture inside.

What's here?

What fits together?

What's missing?

The next pause in liminal space takes you from this sort of accounting arena into the decision-making phase.

What's most important to keep?

What can be discarded?

What problem is the most important one for me to solve?

What elements here are non-negotiable?

Why are they non-negotiable?

Who is coming along or needs help orienting?

As an observer, let's apply this to a story arc that you probably know pretty well.

Golf champion Tiger Woods won the 2019 Masters in a triumphant return from almost a decade of personal and physical chaos. The player we saw there was superficially familiar to us, down to the red shirt and the iconic fist pump he made when the winning putt went in.

But Tiger was a fundamentally different player in 2019 than he was the last time he won that tournament, in 2005. He had been through many devastating physical and psychological trials—many of them self-inflicted. He had broken up his family with his behavior, and gone through a public arrest for being intoxicated behind the wheel of his car. He had a major back fusion surgery and numerous other procedures.

Tiger no longer hit the ball as far as the other top players, and it took hours for him to get his surgically repaired back loose enough so that he could walk 18 holes—never mind actually swing the club.

What made the experience so fascinating to watch as a fan was seeing an all-time great channel the intangibles of greatness, but do it in a way that was compatible with the physical skills he now possessed.

Tiger re-emerged, after experiencing intense chaos and lots of complexity in his life. With help from tremendous coaches—medical, technical and psychological—he became a champion again.

It was a thrill to watch. It was inspiring, which is a creative act of leadership, because we are inclined to follow or mimic what inspires us.

Think back to when you first heard about the devastating infidelities in Tiger's personal life with his wife. When I first heard about them, I believed he was finished as a top athlete, and I said as much to my wife. I could not imagine how unsettling and damaging this news would be to the image that he held of himself. I assumed it would destroy his ability to find the kind of peace and focus on the course that had set him apart. Now, instead, he was an emotional and professional mess and in a downward spiral. On top of the fallout, his body was giving way as well.

All this amounted to a level of chaos to which few of us can relate. As it turns out, Tiger clawed his way back. Over the ensuing years, his emotional and personal life quieted, and in time, from intense focus and commitment, his game began to return. By 2019, Tiger had progressed through his experience from the chaos through lots of complexity and finally arriving back on top of his game as he entered a phase known as self-organization. This is a place of harmony, resonance and synchronicity. His old friend, "flow" had returned after a great deal of work that allowed him to process through the stages we've described.

Tiger was willing to face the music, and learn; which meant he had to cycle through all three of these phases – chaos, complexity and self-organization.

He had to figure out how to swing the club in a manner that was within the limits of his bad knee and back.

Tiger *emerged*. He did his work, remaking himself and his world view. He intentionally transformed into a better version of himself. As he did so, he became a more well-rounded person. You can see it in the joy he gets when he caddies for his son at a junior golf event, and in the stories coming out about how much of a mentor he has become to younger players who live near him in Southern Florida. That's a very different story than the reality he had created for himself a decade ago, when he was a fierce—and fiercely-guarded—killer on the course.

CHAPTER 3 STUDY GUIDE

Executive Summary:

- The relationship between team members is the catalyst for peak performance. That relationship starts with self-mastery.
- Liminal space is a transitional space between the previous state and the state you are aiming to be in next.
- By accepting the reality of liminal space, we allow for the process of emergence of new capabilities to emerge.
- Coaches help coachees navigate liminal space by helping them to uncover their internal motivation and inspiration to change, and then unlock new capabilities in themselves.

Reflection Questions (consider writing your answers in a journal):

- Which of the key points we made surprised you?
- Which were familiar or resonated for you?
- What have been your experiences with being in liminal (transitional) space?
- What was your key insight or take-away from this chapter?
- What questions are you eager to have answered?

Coaching Questions:

- What do you know?
- What else might be true?
- What do you not know?
- What stories are you making up?
- What might an outsider have seen?
- What do you want to be?
- Where do you want to go?
- What is important here?

Chapter 4: Trust: Nurturing the Space Within

"The best way to find yourself is to lose yourself in the service of others."

Gandhi

Steve was going places.

He was based in the United States as the manager of a very large—and previously very underperforming—manufacturing plant owned by an international business headquartered in London. When Steve took on the role, the U.S. plant was in crisis. It was one of the most expensive/least efficient to run, and was outdated. Still, Steve had turned the plant around to be one of the most efficient and highest producing in the company, and was setting the performance bar for all other operations.

Steve was a star, and seen as someone with high potential for a future senior executive role. But he needed to refine some of his leadership skills. Steve and his manager recognized that what had gotten him here would not get him to the next level of leadership. They hired June to coach him.

As is the case in many turn-arounds, it sometimes takes some hard-edged behavior to get something back on track. When Steve hit the ground in the American plant as leader, he was very command and control. He had grown up in the plant and was formally trained in process engineering, so he knew all of its people, processes, and systems intimately. He knew personally how to solve the day-to-day problems his leadership team and their teams encountered, and he'd made no secret of the strategies he wanted his subordinates to use to fix those problems.

Now that the plant was thriving and his leadership team was more seasoned, he needed to shift his approach away from command-and-control. It was time to build consensus and create stakeholder alignment. Steve understood this; he'd gotten the feedback from his team. He knew he needed to back off. But the question was how—because he loved being in the middle of the action.

How would he develop the trust he needed to have, both in himself and in the team that he specifically built for this purpose?

Steve knew he needed help with this, and that's how June and Steve first met.

The coaching process began simply enough. Each session, they would review his week and assessing the specific instances when he had jumped in and overruled his leadership team and took control of a decision.

What patterns emerged?

Someone brought him a problem and he knew exactly what to do, so he'd tell them.

One of his leaders was under-performing and he kept telling them what to do differently, but change wasn't happening.

A response team handling a supplier crisis picked a point person Steve didn't think was aggressive enough to handle the job. So he overruled the choice and picked somebody else.

They would diagnose each situation.

What was the impact of him solving something for one of his leaders?

What were the benefits?

What were the disadvantages and lost opportunities?

It had become clear Steve was the last word on solutions, so everyone brought their problems to him. He was burning out on all the decision-making, and his team wasn't developing the skills they needed to solve their own problems. They started to disengage because they felt disempowered—and actually resented Steve because he was becoming the bottleneck through which every decision had to pass.

June asked Steve to practice asking just one question before offering a potential solution: "What potential solutions have you already identified?" Then she had him ask one more question: "What do you need from me to move forward?"

Sometimes that meant Steve would have to brainstorm potential solutions with his leaders, but more often he found they already had a solution in mind and just needed his approval and vote of confidence to act.

Steve was building a network of trust. And he was becoming a coach.

Instead of coming to him with problems, Steve's leaders would update him on progress in weekly team meetings. He was no longer a bottleneck and everyone's effectiveness went up. The problems his leaders did bring him for consultation were interesting and novel, which engaged everyone more fully. The leadership team started bringing new recommendations for efficiency and innovation forward, and the plant grew even more.

Two months later, Steve's company offered him a new role at their flagship plant in the Czech Republic—which had been struggling. Steve was elated, and anxious.

New plant.

New manager.

New team.

New culture.

New language to learn.

As they started to plan for his transition, they focused heavily on expanding his coaching skills. They knew it would be crucial for him to spend a lot of time listening. What Steve found was by asking thoughtful questions, leaders in the plant started seeing blind spots in their own processes, and solutions they hadn't considered before. He did not enter by telling these leaders what to do to turn things around. Instead he listened carefully to what was happening, asked curious questions to explore it, found the signal and focused on that one signal. Then he would pause, ask more questions, and move on.

In just a month, he had built tremendous trust and credibility with his new team.

They felt safe.

And it was because Steve learned to trust, and not just trust others, but himself as well.

Why is this trust element so important—both for you and for the atmosphere you build as a leader?

Because trust is really the only thing that links a high-performing team, especially in a landscape where so many things are swirling and changing. It's actually impossible to anticipate and plan for every conceivable wrinkle and potential outcome, so the highest-performing leaders don't even try. They have learned that there is safety in numbers, especially on teams that relate well.

Trust is actually a lagging indicator of relatability, or the quality of relationships among team members. When the connective tissue of relationships is healthy, it generates a "safe space" where people feel seen, heard, valued, and useful. Safe space does not exist without trust—which is earned over time from trusting two-way relationships. On high performing teams, accountability begins to take care of itself because it has become the norm, and the space is safe enough that members step in to help their faltering teammates—whether it is to call them into account or simply to give a needed hand.

Most importantly, the sense of trust is not just a team dynamic. As you may have experienced in your life, when you are a member of one of these teams, you too felt trust and confidence in your own judgment and abilities and were able to play fast and with agility.

If you didn't believe this was true before, the COVID pandemic probably made it more clear. One of the recurring conversations we've been having with senior leaders revolves around the complexities of the "new normal" in staffing when it comes to being in the office full-time. I hear so much frustration and confusion—and a lot of saber-rattling.

Let me give you an example. Craig is a senior vice president at a giant multinational tech company in the Northeast—where COVID hit hard and hit early. His company went completely remote in March 2020, and had been making plans to return to a hybrid three-days-in schedule in fall 2022. But a full 50 percent of his leadership team told him that if the company mandated coming back to the office, they'd leave. In fact, competitors in the same space had been using headhunters to recruit employees from firms that are returning to the office by offering not only completely remote work but also higher pay.

Leaders like Craig—who grew up in a stern system geared for a top-down, command and control culture—are learning that the rules of the game have suddenly evolved. Crisis always speeds evolution. True to form, the pandemic acted as an accelerant. As we have all learned, many of us enjoy working from home. We don't want to commute anymore—and as more organizations discover they don't need a large physical footprint and the expenses that go with that, more options are available to the workforce than before.

In the midst of the unraveling pandemic, things are confusing on many fronts. Many of the clients I see come in with a lot of frustration and even anger. Craig's instinctive response when he heard from his management team was harsh. *If that's your choice, I'll accept your resignation right now*, he thought. It didn't get any simpler when he discussed establishing a vaccination mandate in his attempt to make employees who returned to the building feel safer. He got push-back from other members of the leadership team who didn't believe the company should be dictating health requirements to staff.

This scenario plays out all over the business world daily —and not just because of the pandemic. It's globalization, the proliferation of industry-changing technology, changes in the talent pool, market trends, regulation, politics, #MeToo, Black Lives Matter, abortion rights, global warming, international conflict, and economics. Leaders are trying to decide how to draw and live within the new lines, and it is certainly stressful. But it also has the tremendous potential to be a powerful coaching opportunity—both for senior leaders and those on the team.

That opportunity starts with changing your relationship with the terms "right" and "wrong." We're not suggesting you rip up your personal set of values and embrace things that violate your principles. What we *are* suggesting is that the better you become at seeing viewpoints on a spectrum—seeing them as "different" and not "better" or "worse," the easier it will be for you to communicate with your peers and with your team. And you'll become a much better coach.

It isn't hard to see how this plays out through the political lens these days. We're as divided as we've ever been politically, and one of the biggest problems we face is that positions have become so hardened that even friends can't talk to each other without the conversation becoming charged. If somebody is "right" and the other person has a different view, by definition, they must be "wrong." And when you define somebody as "wrong," especially when it's done aggressively, any real conversation stops. In the leadership context, we prefer a both/and rather than a binary approach, which means that there are many right and wrong solutions. Some are better than others, depending on the context. On many occasions, I thought I knew where the client was heading, only to see them find their own eloquent solution that was not within my frame. I love when this happens! It helps me believe in the power of coaching and teamwork.

Think about what the ramifications of that strategy might be in your organization. It might be satisfying in the moment to release your frustration and anger, like Craig was thinking to himself about his team—*fine, leave*! But if you think it's hard to get talented people to come through the door now, how will you feel about having to go out and recruit new people? How long will it take you to build rapport and trust with that new group, and integrate them into the team members that remain? The reality is that organizations that draw hard lines now are going to be the ones who lose. Dollars still matter (as always), but the metrics are changing. Creating an environment where people can be seen and heard and feel trust in the room is the environment where team members are going to flourish.

Charles Green devised a notable Trust Equation that lays out these parameters very clearly: trust equals credibility plus reliability plus intimacy over self-orientation. Credibility is simply whether or not you tell people the truth. Reliability? That's whether or not you do what you say you're going to do. Intimacy is the trust you have that you'll be valued and treated fairly. And self-orientation is the balance of an individual's needs with others' and the needs of the group. If you're command and control oriented, credibility and reliability are often easy to achieve. After all, if you lay down the law and follow it up with an iron fist, you're doing exactly what you said you would do. Coaching helps develop the other pieces of that equation—intimacy and self-orientation.

Think of what this means for you as a leader. At a time when it's never been harder to recruit, where might it be more valuable—and show a greater potential return—to spend time and energy? Getting better at giving orders, or getting better at understanding and connecting with your people by drawing them to you and your organization? You can grow and adapt in this new, accelerated environment, and you can coach your team to embrace the world we have and surf the waves that greet us. You can flow with the idea that learning to ride them is far more productive than trying to stop them from rolling in.

Or you can be right.

To work on this, you can use a specific mindfulness tool we use with many of our clients—journaling. We think journaling is so important that we provide every new member of a coaching cohort a hard-bound book designed for exactly that purpose. We regularly propose journaling assignments, literally, like homework. There really is no wrong way to journal. You might write in full sentences, bullet points, word clouds, or even draw. The intention is to capture your thoughts, process your emotions, clarify and expand your thinking, and spark new insights. It is a great way to develop your sense of self, and with it, increase your self-trust.

The first part is to be intentional about how you evaluate what's happening in your personal and professional life. Consider a specific problem or situation that you are wrestling with, then journal your answers to the following questions:

What am I thinking about this situation right now?

How am I feeling about this situation?

How do I want to feel about this situation?

What do I know? (*Be really precise with this one. What are the facts of the situation? Are they from a credible source? What specifically did people say? Do?*)

What do I not know?

What do I need to know?

What questions might I ask to gather more information, check my assumptions and make a more informed decision?

What will I do now?

Or, we often suggest this three-question short version for when you are in the moment and don't have time to be quite as thoughtful:

What? (e.g. What is the situation?)

So what? (e.g. What is important about this to me? To others?)

What now? (e.g. What will I do next?)

Notice that those journal prompts are also coaching questions. The act of writing it out in the journal can often provide clarity about what is emerging, and give you a sense of calm and acceptance about the changes and challenges it might bring. By being in this accepting space, you're giving off a much more productive energy to the team around you. Instead of being reactive, tense, or angry, you're much more likely to be energized, active, and exhilarated by the thrill of the chase. You'll be more likely to ask curious questions of others, and be open to hearing their responses. This is what builds trust. You'll have a team chomping at the bit to go on the odyssey with you instead of tensing for the anger and stress and threats coming toward them about what happens if they don't do something to your expectation.

Clark was an executive with more than 30 years of experience in the entertainment business, helping huge and complex multi-national real estate development companies navigate the vagaries and politics of local jurisdictions. At any given time, he might be in a meeting with a billionaire investor, a head of state, or an international celebrity. His role in many of those meetings was to be the trusted advisor—and to immediately convey that sense of trust through the room.

That's a tough assignment, for sure, and Clark came to us because he had his own doubts about his qualifications to take it on. After all, he wasn't the billionaire or the prime minister or the league champion or Oscar winner.

We started with a simple act of self-identification.

"Why do they have you there, Clark?"

"Because I tell it like it is. I'm not there to sugar-coat things or convince anyone of anything."

Clark went on to describe the relationship he had with the main investor in his company—the head of a venture fund who is on all those lists of the world's richest people you see floating around. The investor had worked with Clark for more than a decade and had sent him a treasured first-edition book of Walt Whitman poetry he knew Clark would appreciate. On the note with it, the investor had written that he had hundreds of people in his world who told him what he wanted to hear. He loved working with Clark because Clark told him what he needed to hear.

With that "assignment" in mind, Clark's job was to sit quietly and map out the three biggest projects he had on his plate. If those projects were home runs three years from now, what would that success look like for the investment group? What would it look like for the outside and local partners? What would the properties physically look like?

We encouraged Clark to lean into the visualization of what the happy customers would be doing as they moved through the property, and to try to viscerally create the feeling he'd have seeing it come to fruition.

"They trust you to help them do this. Now it's time for you to trust yourself."

FRAMEWORK: TRUST

Think about the way you've been trained to talk about business.

There's a bottom line.

You eat what you kill.

It's a dog-eat-dog world.

You're only as good as your last quarter.

We've been trained to be competitive hunter-gatherers with this reductive, simplistic, binary language. If I win, somebody has to lose.

But that leaves out literally millennia of human development. We're here because we formed collectivist groups—groups that worked together for the good of the "tribe."

Humans run in tribes because we're hard-wired to understand that there's safety in groups. The more efficient and powerful a tribe is, the more sustainable it is.

And what is required for a tribe to be efficient? Sustainable? Powerful?

Trust.

When you feel a sense of belonging and connectedness, you feel safe and trust increases for both the group as a whole and the individual players. My trust in myself grows as others in the group trust and believe in me. And bonding, by its nature, is reciprocal. It is both given and received. We like to call it the glue in a relationship—whether it's the relationship between two partners in a household, peers on a team or a leader and others in an organization.

It is all about the quality of relationships.

We're all together, whether we like it or not. And because there's an unavoidable interpersonal dynamic, we need to examine the concept of trust. To have trust means that others are in your circle. You're not alone. And to be trustworthy means you can be in others' circles. The five pillars of Theory B support the establishment of trust and belonging in a mindful process that helps us to continually re-imagine ourselves as increasingly connected and trustworthy.

In a business relationship, you express that you're having an experience that makes you feel as though you're seen, heard, and appreciated for the set of talents, skills, and tastes you possess. And others validate that by expressing gratitude for your presence.

It is the continual act of finding, adjusting, and experiencing those feelings that creates work people love. Work that matters. And it creates organizations that are responsive, resilient, and attractive to dynamic new team members. Your workplace becomes self-fulfilling and self-sustaining because your energy and your team's vibe attracts like-minded people. Yours becomes a generative culture.

Marcus Buckingham conducted a study for the Harvard Business Review that collected the thoughts and opinions of more than 50,000 people about what they considered to be the key predictors for performance, engagement, retention, and inclusion in the workplace. The answers the respondents gave might surprise you. It wasn't more pay, likable teammates, attractive work rules, or even believing in the organization's mission.

Respondents who were most satisfied were:

- Excited to go to work every day
- Were asked to use their strengths every day
- Had the chance to do something they were good at and loved

That all sounds great, but how do you create the environment for that to happen?

If you're the leader of an organization and you want this for your team, what knobs do you turn or levers do you pull?

It starts with you.

To build a trusting organization, you need people who trust themselves. That does not exist in a hard top-down, law-and-order type organization. It doesn't happen where there's fear or anxiety.

Yes, a military-style leadership model works for.... the military—where you need to get young people ready to risk their lives and save lives in battle where they have to follow specific plans to achieve the mission and support their fellow soldiers. This style of leadership clearly has its place and time, and it is not in the civilian world.

In the civilian marketplace, the military model or even the reductive assembly line approach to managing people is not so great at adapting, accepting and accentuating the differences that are what make business organizations truly great. And these models are especially good at burning people out, alienating them, and discarding them when they aren't needed anymore.

You don't have to look any farther than the Navy SEALs to see this in action. Nobody would argue that the SEALs aren't one of the most impressive, formidable and powerful organizations ever developed. The selection process demands unbelievable strength, stamina, intelligence, teamwork, and dedication. The humans who make it into the SEALs are some of the finest this country has ever produced.

And...

When you make it through BUDS and become a SEAL, the clock is already ticking on your career. Navy operators are eligible to retire after 20 years, and SEALs are held to extremely high physical standards. Very few SEALs stay beyond 20 years, or past their early 40s. That experience goes out the door, replaced with younger generations of warfighters. Operators who spent years building unbreakable bonds of trust are suddenly on the outside. They become "other."

The dynamic is similar in NFL or Major League Baseball locker rooms. When a player is on the team, he's trusted. He's one of the group. But when that player retires and becomes a broadcaster, he enters the locker room the next season as a fundamentally different person. He still has friends on the team, but he's "other."

So the question becomes, how do we take the strands of what the SEALs (or the Yankees or Patriots) do well—building those bonds—and augment them with principles that are designed to create a more long-standing, consistent trust?

How do you create meaning, belonging, *and* durability?

Taking responsibility. Creating a safe organization of trust starts at the top. To build trust in others, you have to find it in yourself. It follows that safe space in organizations must first be nurtured by leaders who are safe and trustworthy.

You have to personify it, coach it, value it, and reward it—not just demand it.

CHAPTER 4 STUDY GUIDE

Executive Summary:

– Relationships built on trust are the only thing that links a high-performing team together, especially in a constantly changing, dynamic environment.
– The better you become at seeing points of view on a spectrum of different, not better or worse, the easier it will be for you to communicate with and coach others.
– Journaling is a powerful tool to capture your thoughts, process emotions, boost your well-being, clarify and expand your thinking, and spark new insights.
– The five pillars of Theory B (Merge, Move, Trust, Choose and Integrate) support the establishment of trust and belonging in a process that helps us continually re-imagine ourselves as increasingly interconnected and belonging.
– To build trust in and with others, you must first find it in yourself.

Reflection Questions (consider writing your answers in a journal):

– Which of the key points we made surprised you?
– Which were familiar or resonated for you?
– In your experience, what builds your trust in others?
– What breaks or gets in the way of your trust in others?
– What builds your trust in yourself?
– What gets in the way of your trust in yourself?
– What is your current practice around journaling? How has it served you?

- What was your key insight or take-away from this chapter?
- What questions are you eager to have answered?

Coaching Questions:

- How do I make sense of this?
- What perspective do I hold now?
- What am I learning about myself?
- Who am I becoming?
- What perspective do I hold now?
- What is possible?
- What is self-authority to me?
- How do I stand in my strength?

Chapter 5: Choose: Building the Bridge

"Between stimulus and response, there is a space. In that space is our power to choose our response. In our response lies our growth and our freedom."

Viktor Frankl

When David's name showed up on the screen of my iPhone, I was almost certain what the conversation would be before I answered.

David was a regular client, but beyond our scheduled talks I would get an unscheduled call about once every third month.

"Dan, I feel like an idiot. Like I'm making the same mistakes all over again."

In a meeting with an outside vendor and one of the managers at the manufacturing company he owned, David was listening to a dialog between the vendor and his manager and got the vibe that his manager didn't think David was making the right strategic decisions about one particular market.

"It felt like a punch in the gut to hear it," David said. "It made me feel like I was failing. And it brought up a lot of insecurities I have."

David had inherited the business from his very successful father, and he felt a tremendous amount of pressure to not only uphold the success the company had over the years, but to add his own signature. He didn't want to be just the caretaker, but to create growth. And he had. By adding several new product lines—including one that brought in discarded materials and repurposed them into new products—David's business was producing record revenue.

But personally, he was miserable. He was afraid that the success was a mirage, and that he wasn't skilled enough to maintain the momentum. That was why he came for coaching.

It's important to say here that what David experienced is completely normal. As you make your way through this book and through the Power to Coach curriculum, the progress you make will not be entirely linear. You'll have surges and pauses, just as you would if you engaged a personal trainer or an instructor who was teaching you how to play the electric guitar.

Humans are wonderful and complicated, and change and progress is messy.

David was experiencing that.

In our role as coaches, we work with many people who get in a cycle—both before they come for coaching and as the coaching progresses. The goal of coaching is to help people notice the cycle and move through it and into growth.

"Have we been here before, David?" I asked him. "What's urgent, and what is the evidence that supports the urgency?"

At the core, coaching is helping somebody identify the space between an event (stimulus) and the response to that event to make an intentional choice. It isn't time in the sense that you need to take 60 seconds or 60 minutes to form a response to a stimulus, but to nonetheless build the skill of creating time in a figurative sense.

It's about noticing and acting intentionally instead of reacting reflexively, and it is a skill one can master with intention and perseverance, which clearly is a strong suit for an accomplished and inspiring leader.

For David, the conversation he was hearing prompted a very visceral response. He said he had a "sunken" feeling, it felt heavy in his chest, like he couldn't breathe. It was as if he was shrinking right before the other two people in the room.

"I felt very alone," he said.

To gain clarity and intentionally bring the felt-energy of the experience forward again, right there during the call, I asked, "What felt lonely?" It was easy for him.

"Take a snapshot of how this feels," I said. "This will be your warning signal. When you feel it, it means you're moving below the line, and you are in danger of reacting from this place."

As you practice this noticing skill, you start to build a very important "muscle." That simple act of noticing is courageous and moves us from below the line— from reacting–to above the line, where we can act with intention.

Instead of reading from a story that has already been written and etched into your deeply- grooved neural pathways, you're writing your own story.

You're literally self-authoring. Making a choice about how you are going to show up in creative response to the experience.

For David, the key was to come up with conscious responses before the triggers arrive and potentially hijack him.

First, he was literally saying to himself, "There it is. I recognize the feeling"

By identifying the feelings, it removed much of the stigma—like a child seeing that there isn't really a monster under the bed.

I asked him what a powerful, productive response might look like instead. He thought about it for a second, and described a straightforward interaction where he was clear about his expectations and where he stood and was able to take a beat and check where he was emotionally before going into an extended response in the conversation. The interactions had the exact value and weight they should have—nothing more and nothing less.

"What does that feel like?" I asked him.

"It feels light. Good," David said.

His posture naturally straightened and his shoulders relaxed. His breathing slowed down.

"Take another snapshot right now. How you feel. How your body feels. How you're breathing," I said.

As David relaxed into his chair, I told him about an amazing podcast episode I had heard by Krista Tippett, where she interviewed writer and Duke University Professor Kate Bowler about her experience as a survivor of stage-four colon cancer. Bowler described the incredible gift she received from one doctor who came by each day during her treatment and asked her about what the best ten minutes of her day felt like. He ran her through this loop of positivity—re-experiencing those feelings of comfort, relief, and gratitude, however fleeting—over and over.

It became a fundamental part of her "practice."

And like anything worth doing, it took practice for David to accomplish this shifting. But the unscheduled calls became less frequent, and after a year, they stopped.

This is how we build the bridge from stimulus to response. We call this self-authoring process a leadership superpower, because developing it gives you the ability to literally watch yourself think, notice, shift, and get a great response instead of the same, less-than-optimal reaction. Instead of going into fight-or-flight mode in a crisis or other high-stress situation, you come into it from a place of control, curiosity, and possibility.

What's there?

What's happening?

What are you seeing/feeling?

What's better?

What can you do?

What can you change?

You might notice that all of the above questions are "what" questions, and not "why" questions. When you ask yourself–or a coachee–"what" instead of "why," you can get to the process instead of getting caught up in the potential to judge yourself or be judged by others.

Remember the story I told you in Chapter 3, about my father and his lack of patience–and how it made me shrink? That learned behavior tracked me deep into my adult years. When business associates would react to something in a way I didn't expect or understand, it would scare me and I'd become defensive and even aggressive.

Automatically.

It strained relationships because they'd become confused or turned off by my emotional responses.

As I learned more from a number of mindful practices and life itself, as well as being coached, I started to pay more attention to how those feelings showed up–and when. Soon enough, I was able to identify the moment and ask myself those important questions.

First I would notice and say to myself - "There it is!" Something is happening here. What is it?

What can I learn from it?

Most importantly, instead of becoming triggered by those interactions, I began becoming curious and, in time, stimulated by them—because they usually indicated something new, important and exciting was coming my way.

What's happening out there? Trust yourself.

What are others reacting to?

What more is there to see?

How can I help us to take advantage of what is happening?

What can I do to help everyone to take advantage of the moment?

The stakes are enormous.

The only way to fully understand the context around your organization and see which variables are the ones that matter–and to create sustainable and satisfying growth not just for yourself but for the members of your team–is to understand yourself.

When you self-author, you're formulating the story you tell—and believe—about yourself, others and the world around you. When you author that authentic story about yourself—and you communicate it consistently and effectively to your team—you create the conditions that separate mediocre, mercenary organizations from high-performing, close-knit, and healthy ones. You move from self-authoring to self-architecting. You're creating meaning in your life—and taking the specific steps to build the life you want for yourself, your organization and your groups.

What does the step between self-authoring and self-architecting look like?

Take Jonathan, a second-generation CEO who grew up with a literal front-row seat for practical lessons in leadership and organizational behavior. Even with that experience, he has always had a passion for both building a better culture in his own company and understanding the broader principles in leadership. Jonathan is an avid reader, an animated, well-informed conversationalist, and one of the more receptive clients we've coached.

If a concept or strategy could help, he was ready to hear it, study it, and implement it.

As we've previously discussed, mindfulness practice has become more popular in recent years—and it's easy to understand why. The science is overwhelmingly clear: Practicing mindfulness through meditation or other similar modalities gives a person a more substantial connection between the mind and body. This self-awareness almost always produces calmness, growth and connection to self and others.

So Jonathan decided to add a quiet room to his very expensive high-rise office space. That way, his team could get all of the benefits we've been discussing here.

But when I asked Jonathan if anybody was using the room, he chuckled nervously and shook his head. And when I asked him if *he* was using it, he gave the same answer.

If Jonathan was encouraging his team members to unplug and recharge in the quiet room, but he was still modeling behavior that consciously and subconsciously reinforced the traditional "grind it out as late as necessary" culture that is so pervasive in business, what story did that tell? What was he actually modeling?

No matter how much you say you want better for yourself and your team, if you don't live it publicly, it creates a palpable dissonance within the organization. It hurts the potential for the necessary trust that exists in truly high-performing organizations.

Contrast that with another client, Jacqui Lewis, who established and ran the American division of Audley Travel, a large multi-national travel agency. Jaqui also had a quiet room in her Boston office. She regularly, at the same time of day, took 15-minutes out of her day to relax and meditate. I asked if she did so alone, and with a surprised glance she said "No! We usually have between 15 and 30 people join us."

This was simply a genuine part of her life; one that brought great pleasure while making her better with herself and the people around her. Given how powerful and positive it was for her, there was no question in her mind she should share it with others. Jacqui, who died in 2019 from a very rare cancer, had a wonderful combination of traits and skills that made up an unconventional and extremely effective leader. She was fierce, powerful, and openly passionate, and she didn't mince words. She didn't need to because she led in an environment of trust and love—and she was one of the kindest people I've ever met.

One of the big misconceptions about coaching is that the coach should be telling the coachee exactly what to do. That often comes from coachees conflating the coaching we do with the coaching somebody does for a sport. You see somebody like Nick Saban or Bill Belichick on the sidelines at a football game yelling at people about what to do and where to go and it's natural to conclude that successful coaching has that component to it.

We disagree, particularly when it comes to the kind of coaching that not only helps leaders grow but also infuses an organization with a culture of belonging.

Jacqui used this gift expertly. If you were not meeting expectations or simply being confusing or reactive, she'd ask, "Help me understand what is going on with you?" If you are telling yourself stories that don't not serve the situation, few questions can redirect you more than this one.

Our most successful relationships look like a sounding board. The goal of the coaching is to reflect what a coachee is thinking, feeling and experiencing back onto themselves and offering a safe space to consider what exactly they think, feel and experience. Is it true and is it serving me?

The tools you're learning in the book are the ones coaches use to help coachees move successfully on the journey of "curation"—examining and evaluating themselves and coming to a personal solution.

A good coach helps you evaluate yourself and take responsibility for your own journey. A good coachee does just that—owns what they think, feel and do.

This is important to say out loud, because before any of us can successfully interact with the world at large over the long term, we have to come to an understanding about our individual selves. We have to examine what we think—because as soon as we believe what we think, it becomes our reality. Which means that if we're thinking—and acting upon—something ill-considered, wrong-headed, or at odds with our basic sense of morality and fair play, the road gets exponentially tougher.

If you aren't getting the results you want, chances are it's because you aren't thinking about things in a way that gives you the best chance to self-author or self-architect authentically.

How does this play out in real life? This is what coaching helps coachees do:

1. Notice those internal stories and details
2. Shift the perspective and narrative as necessary
3. Choose the preferred outcome and next best action
4. Evaluate

Let's examine a coaching session that led to a client successfully going through this process.

Andrew was a talented and hard-working general counsel who had been in a corporate position for more than 15 years. In addition to being beloved by his team, he was an incandescent leader through a particularly complicated period in his organization. The team was missing some key players, and not only was Andrew the point person for finding those important replacements, but was also taking on a lot of work for himself.

The combination of the relentlessness of the workload and, frankly, the repetitiveness of his work was grinding Andrew down. He was losing the joy he used to have for his profession. He was distracted, bored and increasingly disengaged—even within the relationships with his most trusted lieutenants.

Andrew knew something wasn't right, so he sought out a coach to help him find the missing pieces. He was upfront about his passion draining away, but at his core, Andrew was a private guy who didn't like to share information about his personal life. June sensed there was something there, but it took time to build the rapport that would let him reveal his real self.

After a few sessions, June finally asked him a question that proved to be the key that unlocked the door.

"What else is there, Andrew?"

He paused.

After almost a minute of silence, he revealed that his adult daughter was going through cancer treatments while one of his grandchildren was simultaneously going through harrowing surgeries to try to correct a birth condition.

Andrew was good enough at his work that he knew he could phone things in and still do enough to get by. But that would not be true to himself. As it was starting to happen, he felt a tremendous sense of shame and guilt.

The signal was there for Andrew. It was telling him he needed to realign his life so that it served his priorities. But that was understandably scary. He had spent a whole career building to get to the position he was in. Was it for nothing? Was it OK to just turn around and change? What would that even look like?

As we talked through the responsibilities he wanted to balance and the causes he wanted to support, his thinking became clearer and more organized. We emphasized the importance of creating quiet time for reflection, and Andrew got back to making the long daily runs he found to be so cathartic.

Andrew decided it was time to step away from his position and move to a new phase, where he had time to spend with his family, focus on charitable work, and pursue some investments part-time. He chose a different wave to surf. He knew from the start that this would require some complicated—and sometimes painful—conversations with his team and with his family. But we coached specifically around the facets of this plan.

What was the best strategy to build a bridge from where he was to where he wanted to be? How would he communicate this with his executive team? How could he be an asset to the organization during the transition—from helping find and train a successor to staying connected as a wise and experienced consultant so his institutional knowledge didn't disappear?

By leaning into this process and embracing it, he modeled a life without constraints to his team and to his family. He showed that connecting sincerely and openly to his true self was an energy-producer—and that the inherent risks doing that weren't really risks at all.

Why?

Because doing nothing is risky! Trying to hold on to elements that don't work anymore or recreate scenarios from years and decades past is no guarantee or hedge against risk! If you accept that turbulence and risk are inevitable, you can choose to be open and grow from whatever comes at you, or you can live a life where you withdraw and contract.

Which paradigm do you think produces the teams with the most satisfied, engaged, dynamic members?

This reality often presents one of the stiffest challenges genius entrepreneurs will face. You can have the remarkable gift of being able to see something in your mind that you want to bring to life—something that might not have ever existed! And you can demonstrate the technical prowess, relentless drive, and strategic virtuosity to make that dream happen.

But if you don't have this piece—this ability to get outside yourself and watch yourself think—you'll never be able to scale beyond yourself. You won't be able to build the network of trust and fertilization of creativity that makes something even grander and more satisfying than one mind can conjure up.

Another challenge? Many leaders end up being cut off from their teams as layer upon layer of managers and committees pile up. As that happens, team members feel unseen, like their contributions don't really matter. One particularly graphic example? June was coaching the president of a large financial institution who wanted to build a more inclusive culture where team members felt safe enough to speak up about inappropriate sales practices. After two years of hard work on this initiative, even the confidential reporting line set up for these calls had gone unused. June's client could tell from risk management and audit reports that the unethical behavior was still happening. But nobody was willing to speak up.

Why?

Through more coaching, she discovered that the multiple layers of staff she had in her office were insulating her from wasting time—but also from hearing the truth. Her administrative assistants were filtering emails and handling requests that seemed less critical from other leaders in the organization. Some of those conversations initiated by those team members were exactly the courageous truth telling the president was hoping to hear—but not only was it not getting to her, it left those team members feeling completely unheard because nothing changed.

In short, the way her day-to-day had evolved, she wasn't in a position to get the real stimulus and real "raw material" she needed to build not only a successful, emerging team, but a successful and emerging *her*. The "protections" were actually stunting her development—in addition to creating an unnecessary wedge between her and her team.

The president immediately changed her communication policy and required a weekly report of who reached out to her with contact information. Whenever she had a few spare minutes, she'd call one of the people on the list and check in.

Was the issue that was on your mind being addressed?

What more could we be doing?

What kinds of things are we doing right?

What would you do differently?

At first, some team members didn't even believe it was her calling. But over time, the word spread and she started hearing the real stories she was hoping to foster. She also used her coaching skills to work with her team on how to influence peers and direct reports more effectively to make changes toward more appropriate sales behavior. Coaching helped her break through the assumptions she had been making about how she was supposed to operate as an executive, and bringing down those barriers made the company both more profitable and more attractive as a place to work.

By the time a person finishes an MBA at a top program (and again, this is NOT a criticism of business school training) he or she feels supremely equipped to deconstruct the data, find the areas of excess, and make the changes that will transform the numbers on the spreadsheet.

And of course the finances are important!

But the interpersonal team development aspect of an organization is where the potential for exponential growth is. If you create a team of people who are thriving both as coaches and coachees, you create an organization that can grow beyond what you can even forecast.

Think back to the last time when you might have watched the classic Oliver Stone film *Wall Street*. That movie is almost 40 years old now, and some of the scenes are downright hilarious in how out-of-date they are–like the scene when Michael Douglas' Gordon Gekko uses a gigantic, primitive cell phone on the beach. That device was the height of luxury and convenience in the mid-1980s. But now, we all have supercomputers in our pockets!

Just like Gordon Gekko's big phone, his attitude about running an office—controlling it from the top down, like a dictator—is just as out of date. For most organizations, more revenue, more profits, and more clients are the coin of the realm. And "leadership" gets boiled down to whatever the next alpha Ivy League grad decides is the most important metric.

The reality is that anybody can come up with quant solutions. Anybody can make top-down, brute-force demands that trade on fear and pain avoidance. But those management styles are ultimately doomed to obsolescence, because the best they can hope to achieve is exactly what the leader demands.

You get what you ask for.

The future of leadership is building a culture that provides everyone in the organization an opportunity to continually grow, adapt and to differentiate into an A-player. Leading an organization like this means we're flowing and adapting with an ever-changing environment, coaching others in a way that seeds the entire organization with a self-organizing culture, and creating work that people love.

It's an organization that doesn't recoil from chaos, but knows it as an opportunity and the beginning of something new – an opportunity to improve, find new markets, and gain ground on their competition, especially when the competition is stymied and slow to adapt.

Sounds good, right?

Almost too good to be true, but I assure you it isn't.

FRAMEWORK: CHOOSE

Yes, we all have different personalities.

But, as humans, we all have the same wiring. The way we contemplate choices is hard-wired into our DNA from tens of thousands of years of evolution. Dr. Patrick Rabbitt conducted ground-breaking research in the 1960s and 1970s on how humans process choices and learn from their mistakes. The primary takeaway? That humans are very good at detecting and correcting errors, but that judgment gets worse the shorter the gap is between getting the stimulus–the option–and having to make that choice.

It would be fabulous, obviously, to be able to dictate the terms of every choice you're presented in your life, and have as much time as you need to deal with them. It doesn't work that way, as you know.

But what if you could change the way you frame those kinds of situations and give yourself enough space and time so that your decision-making process could improve as if you had that unlimited time?

You can!

Rabbitt's research indicated that the best decision-making happens as if there's a committee inside each person's head. The committee might make a bad decision based on incomplete information, but as more information becomes available, continued evaluation eventually gets a person to the "best" choice.

What does that look like in real life?

Consider these two patterns.

One individual is a firefighter. He or she scans the horizon, and if there's a fire, he or she goes to it and battles it until it is extinguished. It's a noble job, but it's tremendously stressful, and dangerous. The other individual works in fire prevention. He or she does the meticulous planning that reduces the chances of a fire happening in the first place. It's much more predictable, scalable work. It doesn't mean a fire won't happen, but if it does, the damage is probably going to be mitigated by the preparation.

You can create the space Rabbitt talks about between the stimulus and response if you create a scenario where you're working in fire prevention instead of firefighting. The firefighting response? A problem or a threat appears, and you have an instantaneous reaction to it. You might feel fear, a surge of adrenaline, or maybe even a sense of hopelessness if the threat is big enough.

The other methodology? Framing the stimulus and response as outcome creating instead of problem reacting. Instead of the situation dictating what you do, you're using a strategy and vision to move with a purpose to create an intentional outcome that aligns with your values.

The frames are fundamentally different, and the leaders we coach who fall into the two categories could not be more different in how they approach problems—or, in the frame of the fire prevention specialists, "opportunities."

When the game slows down (so to speak), it gives us the opportunity to experience the full spectrum of both the stimulus and response—from the energy of the moment to the emotions it conjures up to the thoughts it provokes to the perspectives it triggers—to intentionally direct what we do about it instead of getting swept away by an unexpected tidal wave.

We realize this makes it sound like you can snap your fingers and gain this space and grace. It's not quite that simple. You do have to put in the work to get there— especially if there are some complicating factors. One of the more common situations we encounter is the leader who finds comfort pushing the envelope, seeking risk that potentially veers out of control. That can look something

SELF ARCHITECTING

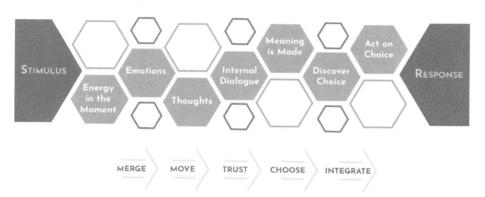

Adapted from the work of Robert Anderson at The Leadership Circle.

like Elon Musk's rash takeover of Twitter, where he ended up spending more than $40 billion because of a series of escalating tweets about how he would run the company differently.

It can be difficult to separate ego and emotion and slow down to actually parse out the meaning of what you're experiencing between the stimulus and the response. It takes both desire and passion to grow and transform and a great deal of mindful introspection. But as you get better at it, you'll find yourself doing exactly what the British say as you get on the tube.

You begin to mind the gap.

What does choosing look like?

It's actually the desired end state we all should get to as we develop as humans. We go from id-reactive babies that demand our immediate needs be met to children with a few more skills to adolescents who test boundaries to adults who are supposed to be able to interact successfully with others.

Dr. Robert Kegan developed the revolutionary Theory of Adult Development that characterizes five developmental levels of "adultness." You move forward and progress as a human when you can successfully navigate each of the levels by becoming more aware of who you are and what your relationship is with the world around you.

His levels?

Stage 1 is the "impulsive mind," which is representative of childhood. When you see something that inspires an emotion or desire, you react instinctively and impulsively. *Candy? I want it!*

Stage 2 is the "imperial mind," represented by your teenage years. The imperial mind has trouble seeing anything outside of self. Your problems are different and bigger than everyone else's, and occupy the center of your universe. At this stage of development. you are controlled by your emotions and thoughts because— in your developing mind—you *are* your emotions and thoughts.

Stage 3, the "socialized mind" represents the majority of the adult population. There, you've been able to open your mind to the existence and needs of other humans. You form bonds and make friends, but your thought processes are still dependent on the actions and opinions of others. You need validation from others to "prove" you're doing the right things, or doing well. In fact, you live for that adulation.

Stage 4 is the "self-authoring" phase. Only about 30 percent of adults ever get to this phase. When you can self-author, you define who you are for yourself—and you understand you have the capability and control to change things within yourself. These are high-functioning people.

The highest stage, stage 5, is the "interconnected" phase. Less than one percent of adults get here. An interconnected person understands that the world is always changing, and that it's OK—and, in fact, advantageous—to be open to continuous change within oneself to move with the world. This is what we call those who master self-architecting because they have mastered the gap!

Coaching can help people to navigate upstream through these phases, and deal with the noise and insecurity that can arise when things get unfamiliar and uncomfortable.

I'm sure you can relate a slice of your own life to those descriptions. For me, it was only after experiencing my fair share of personal pain and learning about coaching in my late 40s that I started paying closer attention to my internal condition. Before that, if I had an interaction with a colleague or a client and they responded in a way I didn't understand, I'd get defensive and aggressive. That would confuse them, and I'd lose status in the relationship. But with increasing attention to what was going on in the gap, I was able to identify that defensiveness and aggressiveness as it was bubbling up. I learned to be ready for it, and in time, I was able to flip the script. Instead of being confused and recoiling when things went sideways, I got excited, moved in, and used the event in a productive way.

Every month, I lead an all-day meeting with up to 20 CEOs. Sometimes things take an unwieldy turn. When they do, I watch with amusement, relax, move in, and go along for the ride. I trust that this group of grown-ups will manage it well with just a little timely help and a bit of humor from me.

Above the Line & Below the Line

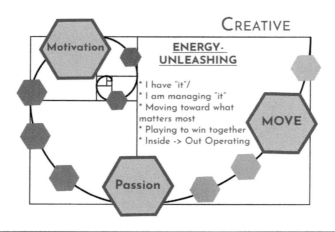

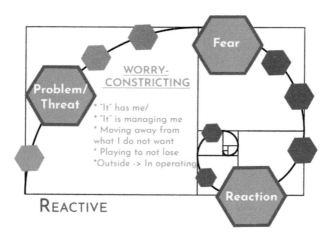

Adapted from the work of Robert Anderson at The Leadership Circle.

CHAPTER 5 STUDY GUIDE

Executive Summary:

- Coaching helps another identify and create the space between an event and their response to that event, allowing time to make an intentional choice, rather than react unconsciously.
- Self-authoring is the ability to watch yourself process a stimulus, notice your automatic reaction, pause, then choose from a place of greater calmness, curiosity, and possibility.
- Coaching helps others:

    - Notice internal energy, stories, language, and assumptions.
    - Shift perspective by intentionally shifting energy as a means of recrafting the internal narrative as necessary.
    - Choose preferred outcomes and next best action.

Evaluate.

- The future of leadership is building a coaching culture that provides everyone in the organization an opportunity to continually grow and adapt in chaos and complexity by prioritizing relationships.
- Progress is not linear, yet doing nothing means you're stuck.

Reflection Questions (consider writing your answers in a journal):

- Which of the key points we made surprised you?
- Which were familiar or resonated for you?
- What personal disciplines do you practice to keep yourself whole, happy, on top of your game, and growing?

- What personal disciplines do you encourage in those who you lead?
- How do you encourage these personal practices in those you lead?
- Can you recall a time when you had a clear instinct to buck the advice of the professionals around you because you knew - better than them - what was right for you?
- When you are performing well in life and work, what is the quality of your experience?
- What can you do to sustain more and longer periods of peak performance in your life and work?
- What does solid social and recreation time with loved ones do for your energy and creativity in your work?
- If you accept that nurturing peace and harmony in your inner world has a direct and significant impact on the quality of your life and work, how important is modeling this behavior/lifestyle to those in your organization who report directly to you?
- What was your key insight or take-away from this chapter?
- What questions are you eager to have answered?

Coaching Questions:

- What scared you?
- What was the trigger?
- What's the energy? Where is it in your body?
- Who am I becoming?
- What do I want for me and others?
- What do I need?
- How do I slow down to go faster?

Chapter 6: Integrate: Bringing it All Together

"Courage is a measure of our heartfelt participation with life, with another, with a community, a work, a future."

David Whyte

So why does all this matter?

What are we trying to do here?

Ultimately, the step you need to take as a leader is to transition from being someone who loves being coached as a means of personal and professional growth to someone who can also develop leaders by coaching them in the moment. This does not mean you need to be a professional coach. It only means that you are willing to learn how to be more effective in the lives of others for the purpose of helping them to get what they want and deserve. It means learning how to connect with self and others more deeply by prioritizing relationships, increasing your ability to relax, listen, and ask good questions.

When you can do that, you've reached what Dr. Dan Siegel calls "MWe" in his book "IntraConnected: Me + We." It means you've expanded your notion of self to include a sense of how you relate to others. It means you've come to realize that your identity is much more than what is happening in your brain. The relationships you have with others and your environment—or lack thereof—are what ultimately shape you!

This can be a bracing realization in a culture of extreme autonomy that works so hard to push the idea that an individual is an island responsible for what happens to himself or herself. But as you have *begun* to see, the truth is different.

Interconnectedness—integration—is fundamental to our existence.

Integration is life.

The best coaching is so important because it guides the process of making meaning. Anyone can push a button, give an order, or point and click. Mechanistically following an order (or giving one!) does not engage all of what we are and can be. Not to mention the recurring theme of overwhelming noise we've been alluding to throughout this book. There's just so much out there now that finding meaning in what you do is one of the very few ways to effectively cut through that clutter and create work that really matters.

Finding awe is a proven means of cutting the noise and connecting to self and others, according to Dacher Keltner. In his impressive research, he identified eight kinds of awe. Surprisingly, the most common form of awe comes from encounters with other people. Call it "common" awe. To experience it, we have to shut off the part of the brain that creates the sense of a separate self. He explains that if we activate the vagus nerve we will shut down the default mode network in our brain, which is responsible for enabling us to create the sense of having a separate self. This means we have to relax, and when we do, we breathe more deeply, our heart rate decreases, we hear better, and we can literally look more deeply into the eyes of others. We will also feel a connection not only to others, but to self and nature as well.

To achieve this common state of experiencing awe with others requires work. But it is work that is magically joyful, satisfying, and healthy. It is the secret sauce for those of us who want deeper and more meaningful relationships.

Not only does this intuitively feel *right*, research over the last decade proves it. When you're fully engaged and connected with something you value, the pleasure centers of your brain light up. Time slows down, and it doesn't feel like work—even if it could be something physically taxing or potentially stressful.

When you feel that connectedness with your work and with your team, that's when you find the level all of the command and control adherents only dream about.

This is something many of the eastern religions have discovered over the years—the sensation of being in the zone or a meditative state where you're aware of what is happening around you, but not burdened by so many confusing signals. But it would be a mistake to brand this experience as something saccharine or overly mystical.

Let us explain what that means.

Clea was an exemplary member of one of the remote leadership cohorts we organized during the height of the pandemic. She was the one in the group who always did the homework and was consistently ready with an interesting insight. Before COVID, she had an ambitious plan to expand her home health care business, but the restrictions and uncertainty of the lockdowns were a shock to her system.

Beyond this uncertainty about the long term viability of her business, Clea had some fears that she might not fit in with the group of other leaders in the cohort. Her company was the smallest of any in the group, and she had only recently moved from being an employee at another company into the entrepreneur space where she was in charge.

With help from the group and the curriculum in the cohort—which is an expanded version of what you're reading about in this book—Clea developed an amazing connection with her peers. She could immediately see that she wanted to build a culture of belonging, meaning and leadership coaching in her company.

That actually manifested in Clea interacting with the leadership group less often, and speaking less than she had before. It wasn't that she had become disconnected from the group. She had just learned so much about herself, and had discovered a self-reliance she didn't have before.

We call that finding a truce with yourself. You're experiencing an increasingly clear signal of where you stand and who you are. That could end up translating into a recalibration of some of the relationships you have, but not in a bad way.

Just different.

A deeper kind of integration is created, one that is based on an authentic sense of who you really are and who you are becoming. It explains why Dan named his firm MindfulCEO.

This kind of growth and awareness is bigger than what we traditionally call "success." It often is what is needed to find success. You can struggle and fail, but see growth and expansion from that experience.

It would be more accurate to call the failure a temporary position, not a definition.

Think back to the 2021 Olympic Games, when gymnast Simone Biles experienced what had to be a terrifying loss of control. She's generally considered to be the best gymnast of all time, and to go through a crisis where you lose confidence in your ability to perform in ways that have literally become synonymous with you— and to experience it in the most exposed, public way conceivable? That would be a shattering experience for most athletes (and leaders).

Instead, the way she handled that experience is the hallmark of what we're teaching in Power to Coach. To be in the middle of something she had been preparing to do her whole life and have the self awareness, strength, and grace to not only acknowledge something was broken, but to step aside personally while staying present for her teammates and friends? That's extraordinary stuff. If anything, the Olympics can actually make us numb to greatness, because it's in front of us in every event. What she did transcended sports, becoming a role model for handling adversity and what so many people experience in their regular, day-to-day lives.

Think about the narrative you've probably just assumed for yourself as a professional person who wants to succeed. What has been drummed into you since your earliest school days? That you need "grit" to win. That if you don't go "all in" you won't make it. But at what expense? In the context of a gymnastics competition, it historically would have meant that an athlete should have demonstrated "grit" and "toughness" by continuing to compete—and putting herself at substantial risk as if nothing else in life mattered.

Kerri Strug famously vaulted on an injured foot at the 1996 Olympics, and the world called her a hero. We had all moved on by the time she got home and discovered that the damage from competing with that injury ended her career. She might say she's fine with the choice she made, but how much of an informed choice is a 19-year-old making?

That's why what Simone Biles did in the 2021 Olympics was so amazing. She was spinning ten feet in the air and discovered she didn't know where she was. She landed, and immediately realized she would be hurting the team if she continued. Despite the stakes and the attention on her and the emotions that have to be a part of that moment, she could see herself and the surrounding circumstances clearly. She was able to accept losing what had been the most important thing in her entire life—gymnastics—because she had developed a healthy relationship with her teammates and her own life beyond gymnastics. Instead of letting it be her everything, she knew it was a part of her life—not her whole life. When anything becomes your everything, you by definition lose your integration with the world around you. You have lost balance.

Another one of Dan's clients, Roberto, is a serial entrepreneur and former high-level college athlete who absolutely thrives on the adrenaline of the deal. The world he operates in is high-risk and high-reward, and he has always been fearless about riding the big, scary waves that go with that. But in between those waves? He was struggling to function not only as a leader in his organization, but as a husband and father. The important people in his life couldn't cope with the damaging behavior that came in between the "wins."

Qualities like "grit" and "drive" and "intensity" can work in the moment, but you can't live there. The intensity of it either burns you out or burns out the people around you trying to deal with the intense energy you're throwing off. Or both. Some leaders and peak performance coaches have started to understand this, and they're embracing new tools that help develop a healthier relationship with work/life balance, achievement, and pressure. One simple example? A WHOOP wristband you can wear that measures how your body is responding to physical activity and stress. It will literally tell you when you're ready to expend energy and when you need to rest.

And what is the benefit of essentially resetting that stress-vs-rest clock? You have the time and energy to answer the real questions that matter.

Who am I?

What is my work?

That's both easier and harder than you think. Easier, because we've become much more accepting of coaching, mindfulness, and some of the other "soft" disciplines that help us discover what really matters to us.

Harder, because we are smack in the middle of an evolution toward a different understanding of how the brain—and mind—work. We've spent hundreds of years using the powers of science to examine exactly how the brain functions. Management theory has evolved with that journey, and we've spent a good century trying to convince ourselves that our brains in our heads are what control the show.

Use your brain, control your mind, and you can control what goes on around you.

Sound familiar?

But we're now (finally) in an age where we're beginning to understand the full science of consciousness. The mind is a broader thing than the chemical and electrical reactions happening in the brain in our head.

There's more to life than just using your brain and your body to go through rote tasks day to day. And there's much, much more to life than your own isolated physical journey from birth to death.

This isn't some attempt to sell you a woo-woo, hippie, metaphysical idea (not that that would necessarily be a bad thing!). It's much more basic and elemental.

Getting beyond this concept of narrow self-definition is the only thing that will pull us out of so many of the conflicts that are tearing at the global fabric. Overdefined sense of isolated self is what fuels the "us vs. them" battles between cultures and religions and neighbors all over the world. It disconnects us and fuels the insistence of so many to treat the planet like a trashcan because they can no longer sense that they are also hurting themselves and those they love.

In our view, our very survival—not just improving results for the fourth quarter or coming up with a better bench for your succession plan—depends on healthy, connected relationships.

What does this look like?

Relationships are the sharing between people of energy and information flow.

The brain is not only in our cranium. It is best understood as our central nervous system, which is laced throughout our bodies, even to the surface of our skin. It is the embodied mechanism for that flow, and the mind is the self-organizing process that regulates that flow—and what you do with your mind can change the structure of your body-brain. When we move ourselves toward deeper integration, we're cultivating well-being. One of the most powerful, science-supported methods for bringing about such neural integration is the practice of mindfulness.

The takeaway here?

Find time to intentionally relax. The options are endless. What is your long lost hobby? How much time do you spend with the people who love and appreciate you? What are you learning for the sake of the joy of learning? What type of movies and books are you consuming? What type of internal dialogue and energy in your body are you intentionally nurturing? When was the last time you helped someone less fortunate than you? Each of these things move the needle, and the more the better. Each of these can be part of your mindfulness practice.

This said, we leave the best for last.

Meditation is an approach to relaxation and centeredness that has been embraced and refined for centuries. We save this for last because it can come across like spiritual dogma too far outside the corporate norm to be useful—which is wildly incorrect in our experience.

Meditation is powerful and of great practical benefit because of its focus, purpose, and access. Its focus is to train and quiet the mind. Its purpose is to give you peace and tranquility and the ability to learn how to live in the moment. Its access is universal. You can slip into meditation virtually anywhere.

The result?

A better life with better relationships living in awe and harmony as we build a more integrated world together.

Research has shown that the practice of mindfulness meditation mends and strengthens the same circuits that aren't functioning when various psychiatric disorders, especially developmental trauma, are at play. As the brain becomes more integrated, people experience better physical health, less burnout, more intentional strength, and greater relational empathy. Physically, meditation and the state of mental presence are associated with optimized levels of the enzyme telomerase, which repairs the ends of your chromosomes as well as the epigenetic alterations that decrease inflammation.

So science has revealed that the mind can change the molecules of the body. But, obviously, the state of the mind is what makes all the difference. Mindfulness meditation helps the mind develop the capacity to be aware and present in the moment, open to what's happening around you and within you as it's happening. Being mindful—being present—facilitates integration and leads to a state of being that's flexible, adaptive, coherent, energetic, and stable. In this definition, we are in a connected flow not only with our own bodies, but with those with whom we are relating and teaming.

Elements of this mental "utopia" actually exist. A client of Dan's shared the following story with us about a trip he had taken to Namibia.

A group of us recently took a trip to Namibia, home of the tribes that have been operating for thousands of years in many of the ways our most distant ancestors did.

One night, sitting around the campfire, I asked the translator to ask one of the villagers a question. "Here in

Namibia, there is drought, famine, and disease, yet people seem very happy. Can you ask why?" My translator posed the question to the villager, who said something I will never forget. He said "We're happy because we belong. We belong to each other in our community, and we belong to Earth."

Then the villager asked the translator a question for me. "Where you live, do you belong?" I was struck silent, and I thought, You know, I can spend a whole day, even in our small town, and not meet anyone I know. There's so little that connects me to others or to the Earth unless I make an intentional effort to make it happen.

It will probably not surprise you to know that studies show people in the United States are some of the most unhappy on the planet—even though we're richer, have more food, and own more stuff than the citizens of any other country. It is not surprising that we are also a nation that values personal autonomy more than any other. This disconnect is increasingly obvious in the nightly news.

The experience of Dan's client in Namibia made us feel that we have a fundamental crisis of not belonging.

Belonging isn't giving up our identity, as many of us assume. Rather, it's developing that sense of connectedness and enlarging our identity to also emerge from the larger whole of the communities to which we belong, which can and should include our places of employment. Belonging emerges with honoring differences and promoting linkages as part of a larger whole.

Which means each of us is a generator and conduit of energy and information flow.

The science of complex systems teaches us that we're all in a never ending process of becoming known as "emergence." Our minds are the navigators of that process—but we don't have the ability to control it or impose our will on it. We need help. We need connection. We need to be a part of something.

What does good coaching do? It helps us to make choices that are in our best interest. It helps us to choose well-being and wholeness with self and others. It helps get us to the next stage of evolution of the mind, and not just in the separate self but in the connected whole. In our business too!

This is how we together can create work that people love and workplaces that are agile and sustainable and where your employees will find meaning and belonging. This is not a pipedream, but an attainable reality for leaders who prioritize relationships by learning to coach as a means of developing leaders around them.

And we're so excited to be here with you.

CHAPTER 6 STUDY GUIDE

Executive Summary:

- As leaders, we must expand our notion of self to include a sense of how we relate to others and our environment.
- When anything becomes your everything, you by definition lose integration with yourself and the world around you. An overdefined sense of self disconnects us from each other, society, and our environment.
- Relationships are the sharing of energy and information flow between people.
- The mind is a much broader and more complex thing than the chemical and electrical reactions happening in our cranium.
- What you do with your mind can change the structures of your body-brain.
- When we move ourselves toward deeper integration, such as through the practice of mindfulness, we cultivate well-being.
- When we are being mindful - present - we are in a connected flow not only with our own bodies but those with whom we are relating, teaming, and leading.
- Belonging is developing that sense of connectedness to the communities to which we belong, including our places of employment.
- Coaching helps us choose well-being and wholeness with self and others, creating agile workplaces to do work we love in sustainable ways.
- Leaders who coach are the future of business.

Reflection Questions (consider writing your answers in a journal):

- Which of the key points we made surprised you?

- Which were familiar or resonated for you?
- What disconnects you from yourself?
- What disconnects you from others?
- What does it feel like to experience disconnection?
- What connects you to self?
- What connects you to others?
- What does it feel like to experience connection?
- What was your key insight or take-away from this book?
- What questions are you eager to have answered?
- What is your next step toward finding your answers?

Team Coaching Questions:

- What do we need to move forward?
- What insights are we having?
- How are we doing together?
- What will we celebrate?
- What could m/we do differently for an even bigger impact?
- Where shall we look next?

Appendix: Coaching Behaviors Self-Assessment

We invite you to take some time to reflect on your own skills as a coach by completing this short coaching behaviors self-assessment. If you are unsure, consider asking your team, peers, friends, and/or family for their feedback.

Instructions:

1. Self-assess your effectiveness as a coach today by circling S for strength, D for development area, and dash if neutral for each item listed below.
2. Answer the reflection questions. Commit to action.

S D — Builds positive rapport with the coachee and actively works to build trust, comfort, and confidence in the coaching relationship; clarifies roles and gains permission to coach the coachee.

S D — Shows sensitivity and respect; understands and accepts individual differences and the unique personalities, contribution, worldview, and situations of others, incorporating these perspectives into approach to coaching.

S D — Works with the coachee to identify their topic (what's most important to them) and the coachee's desired outcomes (not the coach's topic and/or outcomes).

S D — Creates awareness for the coachee through active listening, powerful questioning, and clear, direct communication.

S D — Explores the coachee's thoughts, feelings, behaviors and experiences to deepen learning and create new, clearer insight for the coachee.

S D — Helps the coachee identify a wider range of options and empowers the coachee to choose powerfully.

S D — Moves the coachee toward action through the use of planning, goal setting and accountability.

What topics, emotions, and beliefs/attitudes are difficult for me to be with? What happens when I am presented with them in a coaching conversation?

What did I notice or become more aware of as a result of completing this self-assessment?

To what am I willing to commit to improve my coaching skills as a leader? (e.g. Is it time for me to hire a coach for myself? Is it time for me to invest in developing my own coaching skills?) What specific, measurable and time-bound goals am I setting for myself?

Testimonials Continued

"I have really altered the way that I approach things both strategically and interpersonally. I have gotten more out of working with June during the last 6 months than I have with the ½ dozen or so other coaches I have had combined!"

—Michelle R., General Counsel

"For anyone who wants a coach who has made the transition from corporate to running their own business, June coaches in a very organized and pragmatic way. She demonstrated the ability to meet me where I'm at with no judgment and in a very supportive way."

—Debbie A.Y., Coach and HR Leader

"June is a terrific partner who I had the pleasure of working with on 2 separate occasions. Upon joining Wells she was my leadership coach and helped me being effective in driving the customer centric cultural transformation agenda. Separately, she led a session with my newly established team to identify opportunities for improving team engagement and performance. On

both accounts, June was terrific and made a significant impact. She is an awesome listener, offers timely insights, breaks down complex issues into simple actions, is a straight shooter, and someone you can trust."

—Vikas Mahajan, EVP / COO

"I have an analytical mind, which makes it easy to slip into skepticism. But I could not resist being with a group of accomplished people who were willing to go all in to learn a new skill later in life. Learning that I could actually put my judgment aside, and screw-up my curiosity as a means of stimulating a more open relationship with others was my big takeaway. I am becoming increasingly comfortable not having all the answers all the time."

—Matt Rudy, Senior Writer, Golf Digest

"June had a warmth and depth that many other coaches did not. She also had the real world experience to ensure that what she recommended was grounded in reality. I have been able to build a very strong team from what was viewed as an underperforming group. With the same players, I have focused on a culture of trust and empowerment. Seeing June's mentoring in practice with a team which cannot fully speak the same language as me has been very powerful testament to the leader she can help you become."

—Scott P., Operations Leader

Acknowledgments

This book was more than 5 years in the making, the result of our own efforts and also those of many others who provided guidance, encouragement and fellowship along the way.

We want to first acknowledge the Co-Active Leadership Program that brought us together. Although we had met in a coaching course in Boston some years prior, we had not stayed in touch. It was our time and shared experiences in the leadership program in the mountains of North Carolina - Dan as participant and June as "back of the room" leader - that ultimately lit the flame of our relationship, finding each other first as peer coaches, and then as colleagues and collaborators. Those subsequent discussions were the spark that ignited this book and its companion leadership development program Power to Coach: Develop the Leaders Around You.

With this acknowledgement, we want to call out our clients - the leaders who made this book possible and are the role models for the content of the book. Thank you for sharing and engaging with us. Your desire for personal and professional growth is evident from your courageous vulnerability and willingness to be coached for the sake of growth. Moreover, we are grateful that you also recognized the virtue of learning how to coach others as a means of developing the leaders around you. It has been a true privilege to witness your remarkable achievements, and to learn from your wisdom and courage.

Matt Rudy, thank you for your masterful guidance through the many twists and turns along the way. When we first set out on this journey, we thought we knew what this book needed to be. You helped us see our own stories in a new way and better way. Through you and with you, our ideas flowed and expanded into a much more cohesive product. Your raw intelligence and masterful skill of book writing and publishing made for an amazing experience.

Ted Schlueter, you flipped the script and used our advice on us. Had you not, this book may never have happened. Thank you for speaking up and for being our branding partner.

And, Lina Maria Martinez, you have been a wonderful work partner throughout this journey. Your unrelenting will, optimism and enormous capacity for the work was a constant encouragement. Your imprint is felt throughout this book.

Jeremy Gotwells, thank you for showing up in the knick of time! A book, in today's world, can never stand alone. I was told years ago that we should not write a book unless we believe it will make the world a better place. We are filled with this belief, and now recognize that a book, to make a difference, must be read. However, in the noisy world we live in, getting your book socialized sufficiently to make a difference may well be a bigger task than writing the bloody book! Jeremy, your passion for books and community building is genius. Thank you for falling in love with us. The feeling is mutual.

We are also grateful to our coaches and teachers, from whom we continue to learn many valuable practices and perspectives for a life well lived.

Finally, we want to acknowledge our spouses, Ann and Darren, who witnessed our best and worst selves at different times throughout the process of bringing this book to fruition, yet stood by us no matter what. We could not have done this without you. Thank you for your unending support.

Printed in the USA
CPSIA information can be obtained
at www.ICGtesting.com
LVHW060601250224
772691LV00001B/1

9 781955 342797